How Good Riders Get Good

Also by Denny Emerson:

Know Better to Do Better

How Good Riders Get Good

Daily Choices That Lead to Success in Any Equestrian Sport

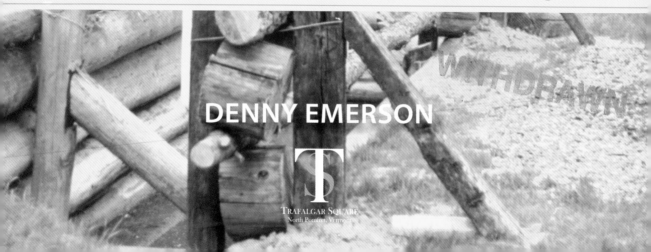

DENNY EMERSON

T

TRAFALGAR SQUARE
North Pomfret, Vermont

First published in 2011 by
Trafalgar Square Books
North Pomfret, Vermont 05053

Revised edition 2019

Trafalgar Square Books encourages the use of approved safety helmets in all equestrian sports and activities.

Library of Congress Cataloging-in-Publication Data

Emerson, Denny.
  How good riders get good : daily choices that lead to success in any equestrian sport / Denny Emerson.
    p. cm.
  Includes index.
  ISBN 978-1-57076-961-0
  1. Horsemanship. I. Title.
  SF309.E64 2011
  798.2--dc22

                                        2010046900

Book design by Carrie Fradkin
Cover design by RM Didier
Typefaces: Berkeley, Myriad

Front cover photos: Main photo by May Emerson; top and bottom inset by Shannon Brinkman; middle top inset by Cealy Tetley; middle bottom inset by Robin Duncan. Back cover photos: Top © TIEC; bottom by Jenni Autry.

Printed in China

10 9 8 7 6 5 4 3 2 1

Dedication

This book is dedicated to the memory of my parents, Edward and Margaret; to my wife, May; and to my sons, Rett and Jamie—my "Support Network," past and present.

Contents

Acknowledgments

Thanks to all who have made this book possible:

Caroline Robbins and the whole staff at Trafalgar Square, for twenty years of urging and support to put these thoughts into the form of a book.

My editor, Sandra Cooke, who patiently walked me through the whole process, and who conducted the interviews of the twenty-three "Good Riders" profiled in the first edition of this book.

My family—May, Rett, and Jamie—for their ongoing support.

The memory of my past teachers—Joe McLaughlin, HLM Van Schaik, Lockie Richards, Sally Swift, Jack Le Goff, and Walter Christensen.

The twenty-three great riders, drivers, and trainers who showed us how "good riders get good"—Sandy Collier, Buck Davidson, Jonathan Field, Laura Graves, Anne Gribbons, Liz Halliday-Sharp, Mary King, Daryl Kinney, Laura Kraut, Leslie Law, Beezie Madden, Sinead Maynard, Scott Monroe, Devin Ryan, Marsha Hartford Sapp, Jane Savoie, Havens Schatt, Louise Serio, Meg Sleeper, James Stierhoff, Roxie Trunnell, Dani Waldman, and Peter Wylde.

Allen Leslie for fifty-five years of friendship and support.

Priscilla Endicott for opening so many doors.

Preface

When people learn that I've written a book, usually their first question is, "What's it about?"

Do you know those vast old hotels, the kind they built in the nineteenth century, with wings in every direction, and halls in each wing, and doors in each hall? Imagine that hotel represents the vast world of horses, and that each of those wings and halls and doors represent choices we can make within that horse world.

A wing might stand for a large choice, such as a discipline or breed. A hall might be who I choose as my instructor, which horse I buy, where I choose to live, and each door I open represents still other choices that flow from the larger choices that I've already made.

This book is about the phenomenon that the choices some riders make open doors to proficiency and great success, while the choices others make close them.

This book is about how some riders are good because they've made *good choices*, and it's about how you can make good choices, too. We all have to make choices every day, and on these pages you can find out how to make the right choices, no matter which horse sport or breed you happen to prefer.

The reason it doesn't matter which riding discipline you choose is because the phrase "good rider" can mean different things to different riders. We tend to judge people through the prism of our own experiences. In a stanza from the poem "Two Tramps in Mudtime," Robert Frost recounts how two loggers evaluated his performance as he split firewood:

> *Men of the woods and lumberjacks,*
> *They judged me by their appropriate tool.*
> *Except as a fellow handled an ax,*
> *They had no way of knowing a fool.*

People judge one another "by their appropriate tool," as Frost says, and in a rider's case, that's likely to be the kind of horse she rides, and the type of riding she does. A Grand Prix dressage rider is likely to think about dressage riders when she decides who is or isn't "good," just as a reiner is apt to evaluate fellow reiners. It would be unusual to ask a Maryland Hunt Cup jockey who he thinks is a good rider, and have him start talking about a rider of American Saddlebreds who shows in park classes. Their worlds don't even intersect.

It is my desire that this book applies to all riding "worlds." I hope you use the many examples that follow to help guide you as you make choices in the days and years to come. If you make them wisely, they can propel you forward toward your goals and bring you to wonderful conclusions.

Denny Emerson

"Wannabes" vs. "Gonnabes"

What Makes the Difference?

Why should I be presumptuous enough to think I have anything to tell you about how to become a better rider?

Here's the answer: I've been involved with horses for almost sixty years. I've competed in trail riding, saddle seat, hunters, jumpers, eventing, and dressage. My primary career has been as an eventer, but I've competed in the National Morgan Show, I've ridden in point-to-point races, I've done endurance riding and completed the 100-Mile Tevis Cup. I've ridden Quarter Horses, Arabs, Paints, Thoroughbreds, Morgans, and Warmbloods.

I've helped win a team gold medal for the United States at a World Championship. I've served on the Executive Committee of what was the American Horse Show Association and is now the United States Equestrian Federation; I've been vice president of the US Equestrian Team and have twice served as president of the US Eventing Association. My Tamarack Hill Farm has stood successful stallions and bought and sold horses.

In other words, in the world of horse sports, I'm quite an experienced and successful person.

Fig. 1 Paint was the ideal first pony for a "wild Indian kid" like me. He was steady, reliable, and most of all, he was tolerant: tolerant of my ignorance, my uneducated riding, of all the mistakes I must have constantly made. I could gallop him all around the neighborhood with just a halter and a lead rope, and he and I became gymkhana champions of Western Massachusetts in the mid 1950s. This photo is from my first competition, April 23, 1954, at the Stoneleigh Prospect Hill School gymkhana, Greenfield, Massachusetts.

I also know lots of people all over the horse world, because since getting Paint, my first pony, at age ten, I've spent as much of my time as possible in the company of other equestrians (fig. 1). The huge majority were "backyard riders"—people who just loved horses, but whose riding skills were no more than average. However, I've also spent a great deal of time with some of the really superb riders of the world, men and women who've become gold medalists and superstars in their disciplines.

I've done a lot of different things successfully in my riding career and I think I'm in a position now to help you avoid some of the mistakes I made along my journey. I can imagine an aspiring horseman coming to me and saying, "I'd love to be successful as a rider, a trainer, a person in the horse world. How do I do it? Can you summarize and explain what you feel is important to becoming a good rider and horseman if *you* were to start over again?"

And I would have to say, "It's not a short answer. In fact, if I really answer your question, you will feel you're trying to drink water from a fire hose. It's more information than you might have expected to have to assimilate."

This book is my answer to that imagined person who's looking for the key to getting better. It's my answer to *you*, if you have dreams of becoming a good rider and questions about how to make it happen.

How I Plan to Help You

I've had the idea for this book in mind for quite a while. In fact, Trafalgar Square Books asked me to write a book about "how good riders *get* good" more than two decades ago, but I was still competing so intensely that it was hard to be as reflective about the topic as I needed to be. Since then my goals have evolved, my experience has broadened, and now I'm ready to share what I've learned. And let me be clear that when I say "good riders," I don't only mean "good in competition"—so if competing is not one of your priorities, you will still find this book helpful.

I have organized the following chapters so you can find the pieces that apply to you. In these chapters, I've defined seven broad *Areas of Choice* that will collectively determine whether you are one of those people who becomes a "gonnabe"—you're going to get it done—or whether you'll be stuck in the "wannabe" category for decades.

Here's what I plan to talk about in the following chapters, and why:

1   **The horse sport you choose (p. 9):** You need to figure out right at the beginning which horse sport you are going to pursue. If you're a Western rider, which of the Western disciplines? If you're an English rider, which of the English disciplines? Are you a breed enthusiast whose riding and competing (if you compete) will be exclusively with one particular breed? Or are you a believer in "Handsome is as handsome does," regardless of breed, color, or appearance? You're not going to get as good if you're in the wrong sport *for you* as you will if you're in the right sport. It's as simple as that. Yes, you can change

and adapt to a sport that's less than ideal for you—but it's easier if you're not trying to hammer "the square peg into the round hole." (Remember this image from a simple toy we probably all enjoyed at some point in our early life, because it's going to come up again.)

2   **The cards life deals you (p. 19):** We all start out on our quest with what I call "life circumstances"—including where we live, whether our family is well-off or struggling, our innate athletic and intellectual talents, even our personality (more on that later). But these circumstances are just the starting point; I'll explain how *your choices* can make them either the springboard to getting better…or an excuse for why you don't.

3   **Your support network (p. 43):** I'm going to talk about how to get along with the people who are in a position to help you, or hinder you. Possibly you haven't realized how large the network of those who affect your effort to get better really is. This information is important because your support network can either make you, or break you.

4   **Your character (p. 71):** I'll talk about your emotions, because how well you control them has a lot to do with how well you control and deal with your horse. I'll show you why some personality traits of which you may say "Well, that's just the way I am," are actually traits that prevent your becoming the better rider you want to be— and they are aspects of yourself you can *choose to change*. It is up to you.

5   **Your body (p. 109):** Here's the physical equipment you bring to your endeavor, the body you use to climb up on your horse. There are some things about it you can't choose to change—for instance, whether you are tall or short. (Your basic physical parameters will also, to some extent, make certain choices in the "horse sports" field more appropriate for you than others.) Beyond that, however, you'll find you have dozens of daily choices that determine whether your body does the best job for you that it possibly can.

6   **Knowledge (p. 137):** Here's a great untapped resource that *anyone* can use to get better. No matter how much knowledge you have, there's always a lot more to get—some of it in areas that might not have occurred to you.

7   **Your horse (p. 157):** I'll talk about your choice of horses because this decision is the one in which you hold the most cards. A wise, analytical choice of horses can put you on an upward path. Conversely, a choice based on a whim or emotional impulse—one that pairs you with a horse that can't do the job for whatever reason—puts your riding on a seemingly endless plateau or even a downward spiral.

How Your Choices Will Work for You

You know that old saying, "Even the greatest put on their pants one leg at a time"? It's as if, in some way, this simple, common trait brings everyone down to an average, human scale. And it's true that in most respects the greatest riders are just like everybody else—until they climb on the back of a horse. Then they are about as much like everybody else as eagles are like penguins!

But great riders aren't born great riders, any more than great violinists, or great statesmen, or great pastry chefs are born that way. I don't think the genetic code that predetermines much of what we become is the key ingredient for a rider, though it may well be the key ingredient for success in some endeavors. (If I'm not genetically destined to grow to more than four feet, eight inches tall, I'm not going to make it as an NBA basketball player. If I am gifted with an extraordinarily high mathematics IQ, I'm more likely to get into a top engineering school than if that gift isn't there—some facts are simply facts.) So don't despair if the "genetic code fairy" was out eating pizza the night you were conceived. There's ever so much more to making it as a rider than your legacy from all the ancestors in your human pedigree.

In my years of teaching, studying, and living around thousands of riders, I've pondered the question, "What do the great ones have that

Beezie was a crucial contributor to team gold medals at the 2004 and 2008 Olympics, and team silver in 2016. At the 2006 World Equestrian Games, she was individual silver medalist and a member of the silver-medal US team, and in 2014, she won the WEG individual and team bronze. Beezie was a member of the gold-medal-winning 2003 and 2011 Pan American Games Teams, and won individual silver at the 2011 Pan American Games, as well. She has 18 wins in Nations Cup competition and 8 World Cup Qualifier wins. In 2013, Beezie won the FEI World Cup Finals, becoming only the fifth woman ever to do so. She repeated the win in 2018.

Beezie Madden on Authentic in the 2008 Olympic Games in Beijing, China, where she won two team gold medals and an individual bronze.

Discipline: Show Jumping

Beezie was the first woman to pass the $1 million mark in earnings for show jumping. In 2004 she became the first woman and the first American rider to reach the top three in the Show Jumping World-Ranking List. She is the only four-time USEF Equestrian of the Year. Beezie added winning the world renowned Grand Prix of Aachen to her list of achievements in 2007. She became the first woman to win the prestigious King George Gold Cup at Hickstead in 2014 and was the first woman and *one of only a few riders to achieve back-to-back victories when she repeated the win the next year. In 2019, Beezie became the first rider to win the $1 Million AIG HITS Grand Prix in all three locations.*

Life circumstances:

My family had horses before I was born. They had a little business: They would buy young horses—hunter prospects, mostly—and bring them along for resale.

Hooked on horses when:

Since I was born or since I can remember, for sure. My family had horses at the Milwaukee Hunt Club when I was little; there was a riding school there. You had to be three years old to take lessons and I'm told that before I was three I would ride a saddle on the saddle rack, pretending it was a horse.

I think I got good because:

I wouldn't say I was much more naturally talented than a lot of other riders— maybe not even *as much* as some! But I think I have a way of communicating with horses, a feeling for what they need: when they can take some pressure, when they need a little break.

My family had gotten to know top equitation trainer Mike Hennigan when I was very young; he leased their stable in Wisconsin for a while. They contacted him when I was ready to aim for the national equitation finals, and I rode from his barn during my last year in the juniors.

One year after the juniors, I went to work for international jumper star Katie Monahan Prudent. I did a little of everything: managed the equipment, taught a little, rode a little, exercised horses, braided…I think all of that helps your riding in the end. Katie really shaped the beginning of my career in the jumpers.

My most important advice:

Be willing to start off by doing anything you can for good people. Sometimes aspiring riders pass up good opportunities to work with top people because they want more of a riding job, and the honest professionals will tell them that they don't have much for them, riding-wise—at least to start with. But you have to learn all aspects of the business. If you go to work for top people, you'll go to the best competitions and meet all the right people and get exposed to everything that's available to you out there. You need to see what it means to compete against the best; even once you're good, you need to keep going to Spruce Meadows and Aachen. Even at my level, if you don't go to the very hardest competitions you can let your expectations or your level of competitiveness lapse.

almost everybody else lacks?" I think I am beginning to see the answer. Recently I had dinner with my old friend Michael Page, an Olympic three-day event rider in the 1960s, and today one of the most sought-after eventing and jumping clinicians in America. We discussed an interesting phenomenon: We've both given clinics year after year in the same places, sometimes seeing the same riders for ten or fifteen consecutive years. Many of those riders never got better, not even a little! They stayed at exactly the same low level of riding despite the passage of time.

I recalled the old joke about asking a wood carver how he created such lifelike duck decoys. The reply: "I took a piece of wood and whittled away everything that didn't look like a duck."

"So," I wondered aloud to Michael, "why can't those people whittle away the pieces of themselves that don't look like a good rider? It's not as if they haven't been told a thousand times how to improve."

Are you a realist? If you really do wish to become a better rider, can you look at that block of wood that is you, and know what pieces you have to whittle away to reveal the good rider hiding somewhere inside it?

If you truly are going to be a better rider, it will happen because, when you're confronted by a choice, as much as possible that goal will guide you. In the chapters that follow are dozens of examples of little choices, medium choices, and huge ones that will collectively determine whether the "wannabe" within you can turn into a "gonnabe."

As an integral part of this book, my editor Sandra Cooke interviewed twenty-three top equestrians—eventers, hunter riders, show jumpers, dressage riders, carriage drivers, and stars from the Western disciplines—who have attained the highest levels of achievement in their sports. They are real life examples and they will tell you how *they* got good; in other words, they all exemplify "gonnabes."

"Every profile is different," Sandra reports, "but they all have one thing in common: Each equestrian's experience in reaching the top ties in directly with one or more of the crucial choices talked about in this book."

The Riding Sport That's Right for You

2

A Cornucopia of Disciplines

Your desire to become a really good rider all starts with your love of horses, but the world of horse sports is enormous (fig. 2). The *kind* of riding in which you long to excel is what will drive many of the choices I talk about in this book.

After all, the love of horses isn't something that most people choose. More often, it chooses them. We all know people who were born into horsey families, but who just weren't interested, and so took soccer or swimming over riding as they got old enough to choose. Conversely, there are stories without number of now-famous riders from families that never had horses, and whose members were mystified when their child's experience at a pony ride or summer camp blossomed into full-on horse mania.

Most people think that some of the things that they do, or the beliefs that they hold, are matters of actual choice, but the reality is, the initial "choice" is often thrust upon them by circumstance. Most Americans are either Democrats or Republicans, and the chances are good that they have chosen the party that was the "choice" of their family growing up. Not always, certainly, but more often than not. The same thing is apt to be true of their allegiance as a fan to the local professional sports team. Most New

Fig. 2 Give your child that first pony ride at your own risk. My mother thought, no doubt, that she was just giving me a nice treat on my seventh birthday. She might just as well have "mainlined" me on heroin. It probably would have been cheaper, and much safer. This was at Benson's Wild Animal Farm, Hudson, New Hampshire, August 20, 1948.

Englanders that I know like the Boston Red Sox, the Boston Celtics, and the New England Patriots. They were indoctrinated early (probably by some benevolent uncle who crammed a tiny Red Sox hat onto their tiny head).

So why should this "choice by osmosis" be any different when it comes to your choice of what horse breed to fall in love with, or what style of riding you take up? If your mother rode hunters and your friends rode hunters, and the local barn where you learned to ride was a hunter barn, the odds are great that you became a hunter rider, too. If you grew up on a ranch in Idaho, and all your friends were barrel racers, it's far more likely that you automatically gravitated toward barrel racing than toward steeplechasing.

If not from your environment, the impetus toward a certain horse sport might have come from books that you read, or movies that you watched, like *Sylvester* and *International Velvet*. You might have gone to watch the Rolex Kentucky Three-Day Event, or the Cheyenne Frontier Days Rodeo, or Dressage at Devon, or the Grand National Morgan Horse Show—or you might have seen the finish at the Tevis Cup Endurance Race. All these are heady influences on an already horse-crazy youngster, and any one of them can lead you down a particular path. After a while it seems to be your only possible path, so that eventually your choice seems fixed in stone.

I think that most of us, especially if we've been involved with horses from childhood, have probably never strayed too far from the kind of riding we started with, nor have we switched from the breed that first captured our allegiance.

I have many friends from my Morgan days (now fifty years ago) who still have Morgans. They still go to Morgan shows where they ride in the same kinds of classes as they did in 1957. Or, if they themselves no longer ride, they watch younger riders showing their Morgans at these competitions.

Similarly, people I met when riding in the Green Mountain Horse Association (GMHA) 100-mile Competitive Trail Ride in the 1950s and 1960s have retained their lifelong interest in competitive trail and endurance riding.

The same people who were hooked on eventing when I met them at my first three-day event in 1962 are still hooked on eventing today.

All of this is natural and, I believe, desirable. We need this kind of consistency and devotion to create structure within our breeds and disciplines, and to provide leadership from one generation to the next.

On the other hand, your initial "choice" of horse sport may just be the beginning. You continue to have the ability to make choices, and your riding interests may evolve as your life progresses. Sometimes the sport that is ultimately the best fit for who you are isn't the first riding discipline to which you're exposed. My history shows that even if you are already involved with one specific type of riding, it doesn't mean that you can't take up another type as well—or even switch completely if you find the new style is a better fit.

My own riding mania started with a fascination with cowboys, due to the childhood hours I spent listening to cowboy radio shows (*The Lone*

Fig. 3 Your starting place with horses may or may not be where you eventually go. When I was riding this three-year-old Morgan stallion, Lippitt Tweedle Dee, for Deane Davis (who would later become Governor of Vermont), it was in 1961 at the Morrisville, Vermont Horse Show. I was working that summer at the Green Mountain Stock Farm in Randolph, Vermont, for Robert Lippitt Knight. Just a month later, I'd watch my first three-day event and switch from saddle seat on Morgans to eventing on Thoroughbreds. (Perhaps your horse sport chooses you.)

Ranger, Tom Mix, Straight Arrow) and reading cowboy comic books (*Gene Autry, Roy Rogers*). It was a given that when I got my first pony, I would ride in a Western saddle. When I learned about the GMHA's 100-mile Competitive Trail Ride a few years later, I shifted my sights from cowboying to distance riding. (I talk more about the GMHA 100 in chapter 5, p. 71.)

During the same mid-1950s time period, I also spent several days each year immersed in the National Morgan Horse Show, which took place in Northampton, Massachusetts—my grandmother's hometown. My equestrian passions stayed with Morgans and distance riding until I discovered eventing in 1961 and was instantly hooked.

When I saw my first three-day event a month or so before my twentieth birthday, I had a summer job at a Morgan farm, riding and training saddle-seat show horses in an enclosed ring (fig. 3). I hadn't a single thought about changing from Morgans until the moment I watched a three-day rider galloping over massive cross-country jumps. Then, as if someone had flicked on a cosmic light switch, I suddenly knew what I had been born to do. And when I became intrigued with endurance racing more than three decades later, it was like closing the circle back to my first distance rides.

Find the Riding Sport That Fits *You*

The horse world is a huge smorgasbord of opportunities, and there's a sport pretty much custom-made for who you are—if you can only figure out which one it is.

First, think about who *you* really *are* (and get used to this important question, because we'll return to it in a later chapter). Are you happy with the order and organization of going around in circles and patterns in an arena, or do you crave open spaces and far horizons? Do you prefer the comfort, security, and discipline of specific and finite limits, or are you more of an "out-there" type who loves speed and adventure and risk?

Do you like to dress up, with every detail neat and precise and tidy and immaculate and shiny? Or are you a casual, easygoing,

James won the Maryland Hunt Cup in 2010, riding Lucy Goelet's Twill Do, trained by William Meister. James and Twill Do amazingly repeated the win, taking the Hunt Cup again in 2012 after the horse came back from an injury. The pair competed in the race in 2013, 2014, and 2015, making it around five out of five times.

The Maryland Steeplechase Association presented James and Twill Do with the Hurdy Gurdy Perpetual Trophy, which recognizes the horse and rider team that demonstrate love of the sport and a profound partnership.

When James Stierhoff crewed for John Strassburger and me at Moonlight in Vermont, a 50-mile endurance race in Woodstock, Vermont, in 2003, he had no way of knowing that just seven years later, his name would join all the famous steeplechase jockeys to win America's Holy Grail of races, the Maryland Hunt Cup.

Twill Do with James (blue-and-white silks) over the last fence and on their way to winning the 114th running of the Maryland Hunt Cup, April 24, 2010.

Discipline: Steeplechasing

James grew into steeplechasing through eventing, foxhunting, and galloping racehorses. His Maryland Hunt Cup victory was his first major win over fences after several victories in point-to-point races. He balances racing on weekends with a day job as a Portfolio Manager at Brown Advisory financial firm in Baltimore, Maryland.

Life circumstances:

I was born and raised in Baltimore, Maryland. Nobody else in my family had anything to do with horses, but my parents were always supportive.

Hooked on horses when:

I always had the desire to do things with horses and would gravitate to any available horse activities on family vacations. My parents sent me to a summer riding camp when I was ten, and that did it. I stopped playing lacrosse and started taking riding lessons. I got interested in eventing and spent three summers as a working student for Denny Emerson.

I think I got good because:

⤷ Not having my own horse while growing up really tested my desire and determination.

⤷ My parents were always supportive; they paid for lessons, came to competitions, and shared my excitement.

⤷ I rode anything that was available. After riding with Denny (on a borrowed horse), I worked during the summer for trainer Bruce Fenwick, foxhunting and showing horses no one else wanted to ride. I learned on a variety of horses how to give each one the kind of ride he needed to do his best over a fence.

⤷ I found a mentor and good friend in Jay Griswold when I started galloping his steeplechasers five years ago, and continued doing it right through college. After a while, I was riding races for him on weekends and found steeplechasing incredibly different from eventing or foxhunting. You have to learn by doing it—a trial by fire at thirty miles an hour. While he coached me on timber racing, Jay also encouraged me to stick with my studies and get my economics degree.

⤷ Because I had to work hard to be able to ride and compete, I was prepared when the call came to ride Twill Do in the Maryland Hunt Cup. He's the nicest horse I've sat on so far, and I was able to get the most out of him.

My most important advice:

Be happy that you're not given everything all at once. If you have some ups and downs, you'll appreciate success that much more. If you can't afford your own horse, remember that if you get good enough, other people will pay you to ride theirs.

James Stierhoff

"kick-back-and-hang-out" type, more comfortable in jeans and a T-shirt? There are riding disciplines that fit each personal style.

There is hunt seat and saddle seat, saddle bronc and bareback bronc, endurance and reining, team penning and eventing, show jumping and dressage, calf roping and team roping, cutting and barrel racing, point-to-point racing and foxhunting.

For instance, if Willie Nelson's Western classic "Mamas, Don't Let Your Babies Grow Up to Be Cowboys" is your favorite song, you'd better get the "Lone Star belt buckles and old faded Levis" he immortalizes in the lyrics, and forget about the top hat and tails found in hunter and dressage arenas. You still have a huge array of popular Western sports from which to choose, including reining (now accepted under the Fédération Equestre Internationale—the FEI—as an international sport), team penning, Western pleasure, cutting, team roping, calf roping, and barrel racing, to name just a few.

If swaggering around in the US Equestrian Team's red jacket with the blue lapels seems like the be-all and end-all of riding existence to you, then you'd better start jumping those jumps!

Maybe your ideal training experience is to be alone in a round pen with a shifty three-year-old colt: As the days pass, you and he find yourselves more closely bonded and increasingly attuned to the same wavelength. This natural horsemanship approach to training and riding has become a booming field, as evidenced by the success of horsemen like John Lyons, Clinton Anderson, Pat Parelli, Monty Roberts, Richard Shrake, Buck Brannaman, and the late Ray Hunt. There could be a place in this list for you.

Maybe your choice of a sport begins with a passionate dedication to a particular breed. There are Paints and Palominos and Appaloosas and Morgans; Arabians, Saddlebreds, Paso Finos, Quarter Horses, Westphalians, Hanoverians, Icelandic Ponies, Norwegian Fjords, Thoroughbreds, Holsteiners, and Welsh Cobs—to name just a few. If promoting, improving, and just being around the breed you love is your first priority, that choice takes you down a particular path of challenges—and additional choices—determined by your breed's organization or registry.

The wonderful thing about horse sports is that you can switch gears—just like I did!—as the years slide by and new opportunities arise, or old ones diminish. There are many examples of riders who've excelled in more than one discipline. Reiner Klimke was universally famous as a multiple gold medalist for Germany as a Grand Prix dressage rider, but it's not well known that in his earlier years he was an upper-level eventer. Bill Steinkraus, riding Snowbound, captured the individual gold medal at the 1960 Mexico Olympic Games; twenty years earlier, Steinkraus had been a champion saddle-seat equitation rider.

Then again, "you" at age fifty might be a very different "you" than at age twenty-five, and the sport you once loved might be too tough on the old bones! Times change, people change, and situations change. If your love of horses has not changed, but other aspects of your life have, be adventurous enough to consider doing something entirely different with horses.

Switch to something you can do that is within the parameters of your new situation. This can be a hard choice, especially at first, but there are dozens of ways that you can enjoy horses if you can push yourself out of that safety and security of the familiar to try something new. And once you have chosen your new sport, you can enjoy it to your maximum potential by using the approach I'm describing right here in this book.

Dealing with the Cards You Hold

3

Can You Change Your Hand?

Are you tall or short? Big or slight? Rich or poor? Old or young? Do you live on a windswept ranch, or in a teeming metropolis? Do you keep your horse at home or board him with others? (Do you even *have* a horse?) The answers to all these questions affect your ability to pursue your riding dreams.

Americans generally believe that "all men are created equal," because it's a "truth" embedded in our national fabric. In actual fact, as we all discover, it's only partly true. Our judicial system tries, often imperfectly, to ensure that each person has an equal opportunity under law, but the word "equal," like the word "fair," is more of a man-made concept than a state found in nature. It is important to understand this, so that we can all have a great big pity party and get our sniveling and whining over and done with. Then we can get on with the process of making the right choices to become good riders.

Life Circumstances vs. Choices

We've all heard them—the thousand-and-one reasons why somebody else has a better deal than we have, and that "if only" we had that same set of advantages, we'd be just as good, and probably better.

> "If I had a $50,000 hunter like Julie, I'd win a lot of classes, too."
> "Must be nice to own a farm like the Andersons'."
> "That truck and trailer the Smiths just drove in cost more than my house."
> "Hey, with long legs like Kathy has, it's easy to stay in balance."
> "It's easy to be brave if you're twenty years old, like Tom."

You may think these comparisons we inevitably make between ourselves and others are life circumstances we absolutely can't control, such as our age, our height, or certain physical liabilities (such as whether we are blind or have vision). We have at least a degree of control over *most* of our circumstances, though. It often depends upon the choices we make.

The hard fact is that a rider's life circumstances can dramatically improve or hinder how far she goes with her riding. As an example, consider the diametrically opposite circumstances of Sally Carter and Andrea Johannsen, both age thirty-two and both aspiring dressage riders.

Sally lives in downtown Anchorage, Alaska, with her husband, Dave (whose company has just transferred him there for three years), and their three young children. She has a part-time job, which she juggles around the pressing needs of her family. Dave doesn't share Sally's love of horses, and becomes easily upset whenever the topic of riding lessons is even mentioned. The Carters are on a tight budget. Anchorage has long winters and is not known for classical dressage.

Andrea's grandfather founded the Amalgamated Container Corporation, and unmarried Andrea has inherited a large trust fund. She lives on a family-owned farm near Baltimore, Maryland, in the summer, and has a condo near Wellington, Florida, where she stables her three grand-prix dressage horses each winter. Andrea is able to work four days a week with her trainer, a noted Austrian dressage master.

Question: Does Sally or Andrea have the better opportunity to become a good rider?

An example of the ironies that we so often find in real life is that it may be Sally who has more innate talent and drive than Andrea. Nevertheless, fair or unfair, the overwhelming odds are that it will be Andrea who has the greater success.

Now, however, let's go back twenty years to when both of these women were twelve years old, and examine how Sally's *choices* have put her at light-years' disadvantage relative to Andrea.

It would be easy to object, "Hey, that trust fund is the main thing that did it!" Yes, it's true that it was not in the cards for Sally to grow up in a rich family, or to become independently wealthy on her twenty-first birthday, but there are many more great riders of average means and modest backgrounds than there are super-wealthy ones like Andrea. Their success is not just a matter of the circumstances they were born into; it's also a matter of the choices they made.

I realize that the problem with hypothetically turning back the clock is that the real-life, present-day Sally would never undo the choices she made, if those choices meant she wouldn't have the same three children and husband she has now. It is not my point to remake Sally's life. My point is to show what Sally could have done differently so that twenty years later she, not Andrea, might be the more successful and accomplished dressage rider—*if that was her real priority*. Her choices might have meant marrying someone else, not marrying at all, and perhaps not having children by age thirty-two. But at age twelve, she wouldn't have known any of that.

Choices Open Doors—or Close Them

Here's the scenario. By age twelve, which is when "horse craziness" really hits young girls, both Sally and Andrea are already pretty experienced riders, although by very different routes. Sally is a "barn rat" at a local stable in Harvard, Massachusetts, spending every waking moment there that her parents will allow. She mucks stalls, sweeps the barn aisle, feeds hay to the "outies" in the paddocks, and cleans mountains of tack. In exchange for all of this, the stable owner lets her exercise the quieter horses, and gives Sally the occasional lesson.

Andrea has had her own fancy show pony since she was nine, and she takes him to hunter shows under the auspices of her professional trainer. Mexicans do the manual labor at her barn, a fact Andrea's parents find normal and desirable. They want only the best for their daughter.

The years in a young rider's life from around eleven to eighteen can be a time of enormous growth and improvement, if hunger and opportunity coincide. Over the next six years, Sally begins to get a distinct riding edge over Andrea, mainly because she is able to ride a very wide range of horses.

But at age eighteen their lives split even further because of some very typical choices Sally makes, choices that start her on a path leading away from her full-time involvement with horses—and away from her riding goals.

Sally has been able to purchase a young off-the-track Thoroughbred. With the help of the owner of the barn where she has worked after school since age eleven, she realizes that she does have a real gift for working through the problems that are so often part of the normal young-horse "baggage."

So great is Sally's promise, in fact, that her local dressage instructor, who teaches at the barn, has arranged for Sally to become a working student for an upper-level dressage trainer whose stable is in southern Pennsylvania, about three-hundred miles away.

This position could well be the "open door" for Sally's riding development, but Sally turns down the offer. And at the very moment she makes *this* choice, other doors that a different choice might have led her to begin to swing shut.

Sally's choice to forego the position with a famous and respected trainer is based on three reasons, some practical and some emotional:

◆ *Reason One:* She would have to sell her horse before going to the new stable, both to raise some money and because the trainer doesn't allow working-student horses. Like most teenage girls, Sally is in love with her horse, and can't bear to part with him.

◆ *Reason Two:* Sally's parents have been urging her to get an education.

She enrolled in the nearby community college while continuing to work at the local barn to defray her horse's expenses.

◆ *Reason Three:* This is the biggest reason behind Sally's decision not to move so far away. She has started going out with Dave, the boy she will marry in three years, and she wants to leave him even less than she wants to leave her young horse.

Meanwhile, Andrea (who has by now made the shift from hunters to straight dressage) goes off to college with her dressage horse. She has chosen a school partly because of its close proximity to a stable with a good professional trainer who can keep her horse in work when Andrea isn't able to ride, and who can give her lessons on those days when she does appear at the barn.

You know "The Rest of the Story." Sally marries Dave and by age twenty-three is pregnant with her first child. Dave's company, a subsidiary of a major oil conglomerate, moves him around the country. By the time Sally finds herself living in Anchorage—about as far from the epicenter of North American dressage as you can get—with three young children, her once-promising riding career just isn't happening.

Andrea, free to pursue dressage full-time, has trained and competed in Europe and has just been named to the training list for the US Equestrian Team prior to the upcoming World Championships.

Your Choices Matter

Although these are stereotyped situations, the fact remains that "life circumstances"—some of which you start out with, but *some of which come about through your specific choices*—greatly impact your chance for riding success.

If you are hooked on barrel racing and you live in Paoli, Pennsylvania, instead of Cody, Wyoming, you are in trouble. If you are an aspiring point-to-point jockey and you live on a horse farm in Middleburg, Virginia, or Camden, South Carolina, you are in much better shape than if

Anne rode Metallic for the US Team that won a silver medal at the 1995 Pan Am Games, and the horse went on to the 1996 Olympics with Robert Dover, where the Team won the bronze medal. A number of her current and former students have competed at the FEI levels, and several have schooled and shown their own horses to Grand Prix with her help. From 2009 to 2012, Anne was the USEF Technical Advisor and coach for the dressage team. During her tenure the US earned two individual medals in the 2010 World Equestrian Games, won the team gold medal and swept all three individual medals at the 2011 Pan American Games, and finished sixth at the London 2012 Olympics, with all the riders scoring over 70 percent for the first time.

Anne Gribbons is a rider, trainer, FEI 5* judge, and former technical advisor for the USET dressage squad.

Here she celebrates a happy moment on Alazan, one of her own horses. Anne has trained and shown sixteen of her own horses to Grand Prix, nine of which were United States Equestrian Team long-listed.

Discipline:
Dressage

Anne is a licensed USEF Senior judge and an FEI 5* judge. She has judged four World Cup Finals, three European Championships, and was the head of the ground jury at the Tryon World Equestrian Games in Tryon, North Carolina, in 2018. From 2010 to 2013 she was a member of the FEI Dressage Committee. In 2006, Anne was named "Horseman of the Year" by The Chronicle of the Horse, and in 2013, she was inducted *into the USDF Hall of Fame. Anne was instrumental in designing the present USEF pipeline for education and development of US dressage athletes.*

Life circumstances:
I grew up with horses in my genes. My grandfather was a head of Swedish cavalry, and I used to sit on his lap as he painted watercolor scenes from his cavalry days.

Hooked on horses when:
I think one of the first things I said was "horse."

I think I got good because:
❧ I couldn't have a horse of my own (my parents and four children—including me—lived in an apartment in Gothenburg, Sweden), but I religiously took lessons at the nearby riding school, where I got good enough to be trusted with some of the greener school horses, and eventually exercised some of the boarders' horses. Then they started giving me rogues that no one else wanted to, or could, ride. I hit the ground often but I learned to stay on. And I got help from the wonderful teachers there.

❧ After I switched to dressage from my first love, eventing, in the 1970s, I was lucky enough—through a sheer accident of timing—to work with some of the masters. Colonel Bengt Ljungquist was my foundation and my mentor for eight years until his unexpected death in 1979. That was upsetting; when I finally pulled myself together, I was able to arrange training tours in Europe with Harry Boldt, Herbert Rehbein, and Dr. Volker Moritz. I look back on all my teachers with enormous gratitude for the experience and wisdom they shared with me. When someone teaches you, that person gives you a gift that is yours to keep and develop, but which nobody can take away. And I feel extremely lucky to be married to David, who always has given me his full support in all my efforts.

❧ I bond with my horses. They've stayed with me, and I have trained most of them up from the beginning, or at least from a very early stage. It really makes a difference when a rider has a strong relationship with a horse; I can tell if there's that kind of bond when I'm judging.

My most important advice:
If you're serious, first of all get a trainer you can trust—not necessarily a genius or the biggest name, but someone you know can get the job done, is interested in you and wants to promote you, and who will tell you the truth and stick by you when the going gets rough. Then, ride every single horse you have the opportunity to ride. *Anybody* can learn to ride one horse. Riding a multitude of horses and figuring them all out—that's what makes you a rider and a *trainer*.

Anne Gribbons

you live in Taos, New Mexico. It's easier to become a good calf roper outside of Dallas, Texas, than outside of Boston, Massachusetts.

We are only partly in control of our life situation at any given time. Some things, like our age, we can never control. We can only partly control our health. But even the things we *can* control, like where we choose to live or what kind of job we get, entail side effects and repercussions. For most of us, life is a juggling act in which riding is only one of the things we're juggling. If riding is high on our list of choices, then other things are necessarily lower and our choices reflect those priorities.

■ A (First Person) Real Life Example

If your location is not where your sport of choice is happening, you either have to remain outside the mainstream of your sport, or you have to "go where the action is"—which is what I did in order to learn to become a three-day-event rider.

I went to watch my first three-day event, the 1961 Wofford Cup held at Groton House Farm in South Hamilton, Massachusetts. At the time I was majoring in English at Dartmouth College and had a summer job at a Morgan horse farm in Randolph, Vermont. But I was blown away by what those event horses and riders were doing on cross-country, and decided then and there that I was going to be a three-day rider.

In retrospect, I actually think I envisioned more than that. At that moment, I decided that I would become a *champion* three-day rider, and ride for the US Equestrian Team. Such is the arrogance and ignorance of youth! It had been less than a decade since, at age thirteen and with zero background in distance riding, I had decided to ride in the GMHA 100 (see page 83 for *that* story).

At age twenty I had never jumped a fence. I knew absolutely nothing about dressage. I owned a Morgan show horse, not an event horse. I'd seen one event in my entire life. Not exactly ideal life circumstances for an aspiring champion three-day rider! But when I got back to my job at the Green Mountain Stock Farm at the end of the weekend, I announced to farm trainer Art Titus that I wanted to learn how to jump and asked him, "How do I do that?" Art's answer: "Put up a jump one foot high, jump it until you get bored, then raise it."

Go to Your Mountain

Remember the story of Muhammad and the Mountain? Muhammad ordered the distant mountain to come closer. The mountain didn't move. Whereupon Muhammad said, "If the mountain will not come to Muhammad, then Muhammad will go to the mountain."

As an aspiring rider, you too, must be prepared to "go to" whatever in your riding sport constitutes your "mountain" (figs. 4 A–C).

You may ride Morgans in upstate New York. The Grand National Morgan Horse Show is quite inconveniently located in Oklahoma City, Oklahoma. Be prepared to pack your gear, load your horse, and hit the road.

You might prefer that the Quarter Horse Congress wasn't located each October in Columbus, Ohio. Too bad. That's why they invented horse trailers.

The Tevis Cup is in Auburn, California. The Rolex Kentucky Three-Day Event is in Lexington, Kentucky, the National Finals Rodeo is in Las Vegas, Nevada, Dressage at Devon is in Devon, Pennsylvania.

"If you build it, they will come." Well, that's where they built it, so that's where you must be willing to go.

Figs. 4 A–C For American event riders, since the late 1970s our "mountain" has been the Kentucky Three-Day Event. Here, I'm jumping Farnley Rob Roy at the Head of the Lake in 1983.

Fig. 5 You can do all sorts of things if you don't know you *can't* do them. Just one year earlier, in July of 1961, I'd seen my first three-day event, the Wofford Cup, at Groton House, in South Hamilton, Massachusetts. I decided then and there to become an event rider. I'd never jumped, never done dressage, basically knew nothing at all about eventing. So here I am on my five-year-old first event horse, Lighting Magic (TB by Grey Flares x Blue Witch, foal of 1957) in a long-format, Preliminary-level, three-day event at GMHA in South Woodstock, Vermont.

This was the beginning of my jumping career. I was quickly bored with one-foot jumps. I'd like to say that was because of my superior talent, but more likely it was because I was a twenty-year-old boy with more ambition and guts and drive than common sense. So I just started jumping bigger fences. Because I'd ridden so many thousands of hours already, I had good balance and no fear. It didn't take long before I felt comfortable and secure.

When I look at old photographs of my early jumping style, I realize that I was a poster boy for cardinal jumping sins: My stirrups were too long, my body position was too far forward, my eyes looked down and my lower legs swung back. But I didn't care, because I was convinced that I was God's gift to the equitation world. It's great to be young and ignorant, two words that I've increasingly come to believe are almost synonymous!

Back at Dartmouth that fall, I did three things to start me off on my brand new career. I sold my Morgan. I bought two books on dressage, A.L. D'Endrody's *Give Your Horse a Chance* and Waldemar Seunig's *Essence of Horsemanship*. And I got in touch with Joe McLaughlin, who ran Hitching Post Farm, a girls' summer eventing camp in Royalton, Vermont, and a thirty-five to forty-minute drive from Dartmouth. For the next two years, I spent every free moment at Hitching Post, riding every horse Joe would let me sit on. If I'd given my car its head, it would probably have driven there by itself.

I also discovered that H.L.M. Van Schaik, a member of the Dutch Olympic silver medal Grand Prix Show Jumping team for the 1936 Berlin Olympics, was living in Cavendish, Vermont—only a few miles from my parents' farm in South Reading. In the spring of 1962 I bought a five-year-old Thoroughbred, Lighting Magic ("Dennis"), from Henry and Janet Schurink. With Mr. Van Schaik's help, I started preparing him for the 1962 Green Mountain Horse Association Preliminary Level Three-Day.

Thirty horses competed, a huge entry in those early days of eventing. Steeplechase took place down in the valley floor, on the GMHA meadows. The second roads and tracks ran straight up the mountain to Lloyd and Stella Reeves' Flying Heels Farm, and the cross-country course went up over the top of the mountain and down the other side (fig. 5). How we survived—a totally green event rider on a totally green five-year-old event horse—remains a mystery to this day, but nineteen pairs finished the event, and Lighting Magic and I were nineteenth.

My graduation from college in June 1963 was the point at which I made some choices that probably "opened the door" to other choices. This series of decisions resulted, eleven years later, in my standing in the arena at the Burghley (England) World Championship Three-Day Event with my teammates Don Sachey, Mike Plumb, and Bruce Davidson, receiving a gold medal from Great Britain's Prince Philip and hearing the "Star Spangled Banner" on the arena speaker as the US flag was raised (fig. 6).

I didn't foresee all this back in 1963, but I'm pretty sure I *hoped* for something like it. What I did know was that I wanted to become a really good event rider, and I needed to figure out how to make that happen. So here are the choices I made.

Fig. 6 There's a pattern emerging here, I realize. What I tend to do is set unrealistic goals and then simply go after them, buoyed mainly by ignorance and enthusiasm. This is the medal ceremony at the 1974 World Championship Three-Day Event, at the Burghley Horse Trials, in Stamford, Lincolnshire, England. As Prince Philip handed us our gold medals, I remember he said, "Well done, boys." Left to right: Prince Philip, Mike Plumb on Good Mixture, Bruce Davidson on Irish Cap, me on Victor Dakin, and Don Sachey on a borrowed Cajun (his Plain Sailing had a minor injury).

◆ I decided that in order to have time to ride, I'd need more free time than a conventional nine-to-five job would allow. Teaching school struck me as the "day job" career that would give me late afternoons off, plus weekends, plus summer vacations—even though the pay was terrible.

◆ I learned that there was an opening available in the English department at Far Hills Country Day School in New Jersey. Far Hills is next door to Gladstone, New Jersey, which was then the site of the United States Equestrian Team (USET) training headquarters for both show jumping and eventing.

◆ I drove down from New Hampshire for a job interview one spring weekend and was hired to teach sixth grade English for the 1963–1964 school year at Far Hills Country Day.

In 1963, the USET headquarters was in the midst of thousands of acres of pristine riding country that was also the home territory of the Essex Foxhounds. Highways, subdivisions, and golf courses have cut into much of the riding area by now, but in those days the whole Far Hills, Bernardsville, Peapack-Gladstone area of New Jersey was one of the premier places to ride in America.

For the next two years I was in the middle of all that horse activity, and I plunged in heart and soul. I hunted with Essex, some days for seven or eight hours. On weekends I could watch legendary coach Bert de Némethy teach the great USET show jumping squad—fabulous riders like Frank Chapot, Kathy Kusner, Mary Mairs, Bernie Traurig, Billy Robertson, and the "the man" himself, Bill Steinkraus, who in just five years would win the individual gold medal at the 1968 Olympics in Mexico City on Snowbound.

The three-day team was then coached by another Hungarian expatriate, Stephan Von Visy. Michael Page, Mike Plumb, Lana duPont, Kevin Freeman, and Jim Wofford were among the three-day squad who either lived full time at the team headquarters in Gladstone or came in for weeks or months at a time—and I could watch their training sessions, as well.

I became friends with Denny Crawford, an avid eventer, and through him, with General "Fuddy" Wing, a former Olympic show jumper and a USET official. Often, Denny and his wife Ailsa would take Lighting Magic and me to events in Maryland and Virginia, where I'd compete at Preliminary Level and Denny would compete his Royal Nubbins at Intermediate.

I raced Lighting Magic in the 1964 Essex Point–to–Point, took dressage clinics with Major Dezso Szilagyi (a product of the famous Hungarian riding school and author of *Basic Classical Dressage*), showed in hunter and jumper classes at local shows, and taught lessons to Essex Pony Club kids, many of whom I also taught at Far Hills Country Day. In short, I had engineered my own life circumstances to further my riding goals.

I recently was able to "time travel" back to those crucial years when I found some old diaries of mine among boxes of effects left in my parents' Vermont house. My entries from 1965, when I was twenty-three, show how totally I involved myself in the rich horse environment to which I'd relocated:

Sinead's second place finish at the 2012 Burghley Horse Trials, one of only six CCI 5* events worldwide, made her the highest-placed American woman in Burghley history.

Sinead Halpin Maynard with US Eventing Team Coach David O'Connor in 2016.

Sinead shows her characteristic focus and determination on course with Manoir de Carneville at Burghley in 2012.

Discipline: Eventing

The first major win of Sinead's competitive career came in 2005 at the National Championships at Radnor. She was a member of the silver-medal-winning Nations Cup Team in Holland in 2010, was the top American at the Kentucky Three-Day Event in 2011, and was the first alternate for the US Eventing Team in the 2012 London Olympics. Sinead represented America in Normandy, France, at the World Equestrian Games in 2014, and was named the alternate for the team for the Rio Olympics in 2016.

Life circumstances:

Both of my parents emigrated from Ireland. My mother grew up with horses and ponies as part of life when she was young in the country. My father grew up in Dublin with little education and nothing to do with horses. They moved to the United States in 1980.

Hooked on horses when:

When I was six I begged for lessons, and my mom was keen on the idea of horses coming back into her life. Over the next few years, weekly lessons turned into a full-on passion, which both my parents encouraged. We were not a wealthy family but my parents believed in following your passion and working hard.

I think I got good because:

↪ I think my parents' influence is a strong reason for the success I have had, as well as impacting my approach with horses. A strong work ethic and a good attitude was mandatory from my mother in the barn—complaining was not a thing that was accepted. My father grew up one of ten kids, raised by his mother and sisters as his father passed away when he was not yet a teenager. He worked every job available throughout his life. To him, there was no time for excuses, just time to jump at any opportunity and see where it might lead. My parents worked incredibly hard to enable me to have a horse. They never told me no; they just said if you can figure it out, go for it. Because of this, I have always felt if I worked hard enough, anything is achievable.

↪ Being a working student has had a huge influence on my life. I started working in professional barns at a very young age. I got to see what the life of a professional looked like. I got to work with beautiful horses, and although I worked for great riders, I also benefited from working directly under great grooms and barn managers. I learned how to listen to and watch the farriers and vets. I got to see how integral the relationships with staff, owners, and sponsors were in the well-roundedness of a program. The quality of the team around you weighs heavily on your chances of success.

↪ Location, location, location. If you want to be the best you need to be around the best. People sometimes say, "You're so lucky to have ridden with the people you've ridden with and lived where you have lived." Luck had very little to do with it. I got in my car, drove to where the people I wanted to be like worked, and I cleaned their stalls.

My most important advice:

You should be able to put your head on your pillow at night and feel you have done your best with the horses and the people around you. If you wake up in the middle of the night not certain you have done right by a person or a horse, fix it…do not become a victim of it. Educate yourself. Seek out help from the people who inspire you; read, write, and believe the learning is in the struggle…and embrace it.

Sinead Halpin Maynard

January 7
Dennis shod—winter (borium tips).
January 9
Hunted from Brady's about 4½ hours. Good hunt—five to ground.
January 11
Rode Sextet for Dr. Lohmeyer, worked Folly, did all stalls.
January 30
USCTA [United States Combined Training Association] *luncheon, NYC. Polo, Squadron A Armory. Dennis high-point horse, USCTA, 1964.*

Subsequent entries chronicle my riding in everything from below-zero cold snaps to February mud. On a late-March trip to Southern Pines with Dennis, I also rode every other horse that crossed my path, including a green colt that bucked me off. By summer, Dennis and I were going intermediate in eventing, and I was also competing him in dressage and show jumping.

When I looked through those old journals recently, I had few active memories of the nonstop riding and learning experiences they chronicled—but I was a horse fanatic, pure and simple. And I was laying the foundation for my future career.

Work to Ride vs. Ride for Work

Many aspiring riders find themselves in this dilemma: They love to ride and desperately want to own a horse, but are so financially strapped that they decide to get a job outside the horse industry that pays enough to enable them to afford to own a horse, pay board, take lessons, and compete.

Others will grind away at even the most menial, low-paying jobs within the horse industry just to have the chance to live their life in immediate proximity to horses.

In my experience, the second choice is the best kind of job for an aspiring rider: some sort of job in the horse industry that lets you ride, even if the job is low-paying and heavy on the manual labor end. This might mean anything from stall-cleaning flunky, barn manager, groom, or

George Morris: The Right Place, the Right Time

For as long as I can remember, George Morris has been a defining figure in American horse sport, as rider, teacher, trainer, author, and Olympic gold medal coach.

I was having lunch with him recently, and he told me that when he was a little boy growing up in the late 1940s through the 1950s, his "life circumstances" were quite perfectly aligned to provide him with a huge edge on his path to greatness. ("Greatness" is my word, not his.)

Using a napkin as an impromptu map, George put his finger on a spot. "This is New York City." Then he traced a half circle to the left of that spot. "And this is Westchester County, where I grew up. That's where riding education 'was' in the 1950s—Gordon Wright, all the great instructors."

George then traced a curve to the right. "That's Long Island. Great foxhunting and riding, but not the best teachers, except for Vladimir Littauer.

"And, down here in New Jersey, there was good riding and showing, but not great instruction."

George went on to list others who came of age at about the same time in about the same quite small geographical area: Bill Steinkraus, Ronnie Mutch, Victor Hugo-Vidal, Jessica Newberry, and Patty Heukeroth.

He added, "If my family had lived an hour north, instead of right there…" He shrugged his shoulders and raised his eyebrows as if to ask, "Who knows what might have become of me?"

Knowing George's drive and genius, I believe he'd have forged his own destiny in any case, but certainly his advantageous early life circumstances made his initial choices easier.

assistant trainer, to trainer and professional rider. In this type of job situation, you really are "killing two birds with one stone." But don't expect that you will easily find a *riding* job, where the barn owner wants you to ride everything on the farm—at least not right away. That may come later,

The first and only woman to win the National Reined Cow Horse Association's Snaffle Bit Futurity Championship, Sandy was inducted into the Cowgirl Hall of Fame in 2011 and the NRCHA Hall of Fame in 2012.

"It's always such a journey working with each individual horse and finding out what they want to excel at," says top reiner and reined cow horse trainer Sandy Collier. "I can't imagine anything I'd rather do!"

Disciplines: Reining/Reined Cowhorse

Named one of the "Top 50 Riders of All Time and All Disciplines" by Horse & Rider Magazine in 2011, Sandy has won numerous major championships, including the NRCHA Stallion Stakes and the Cowhorse Classic Futurity. She is also an NRCHA AAA judge.

Life circumstances:

I was born into a suburban New York family that did the country club thing—golf and tennis. My mother and her mother had ridden horses but they weren't really horse people.

Hooked on horses when:

I always tell people this love affair with horses began when my cells started to divide. I rode in my first horse show at age six.

I think I got good because:

🐾 When my mother realized I was absolutely a horse person, she made sure I got lessons with quality trainers and helped me get involved with Pony Club and eventing (because that's what was available in our area). That was my foundation; the seat I developed for dressage contributed to my success as a reiner.

🐾 I moved out West at age nineteen and developed a "Renaissance" focus that got me involved with all aspects of horses. I was breaking wild mustangs and packing horses into Los Padres National Forest; I learned to shoe, braid rawhide, make saddles, and do a lot of vet work. I brought all that expertise to bear when I became enamored of working cow horses in my twenties.

🐾 I've always wanted to excel at whatever interests me, so I'm forever tapping into anyone who I think does something better than I do. I rode cow horses non-professionally for a year under the tutelage of Doug Ingersoll before turning pro. So many people have helped me since that beginning, I can't single anyone out. Some of them don't even know they've helped me, because I just learned by watching them.

🐾 I've always worked seven days a week and had this insatiable desire to learn that kept propelling me to higher levels of competition.

My most important advice:

You can't dabble; you need to immerse yourself. If this is truly your passion, you will jump out of bed every day *craving* to go straight to the barn and get on your horse. Find a professional whose whole life—not just his riding style but his ethics, how he works with people—you emulate, and dive in with both feet. If you can't be there all the time, be there whenever you can, help out, and ride any horse you can. When you learn a new skill, solidify it in your mind by helping others to learn it. Plan on working "366" days a year. Finally, understand that if a horse isn't "getting" something you are asking him to do, *you* are the problem—not the horse.

Sandy Collier

when you've acquired more skills. Early mornings and lots of stall cleaning are more the entry-level norm!

Why take this route? The hard fact is that those riders who opt for the most financially sensible choice—the better-paid day job apart from horses—automatically remove themselves from all kinds of interactions with horses.

They won't learn as much about feeding, clipping, bandaging, turnout, shoeing, and the thousand-and-one aspects of general horse management that those who work all day, every day with horses absorb almost by osmosis.

And *they won't be there every time a horse needs to be ridden.* It's this aspect—saddle time—that begins to give the full-time horse person the greatest edge over his or her more financially secure and sensible counterpart.

Whatever your job, you can usually concoct some situation that lets you ride if you want it badly enough. If you can't juggle your job around to make horses fit into your life, you might seriously consider a different job. In other words, if you really want to ride and the circumstances in which you find yourself seem to be a conspiracy to prevent you from riding, you either accept that your riding will have to be on the back burner, at least for now, or you have to start changing your circumstances. One of the first places to start is to carefully evaluate your current job. Some jobs own you, and some give you considerable flexibility. I'll return to my own history for some examples of what I mean.

■ Shaping Life around Riding

By 1969, I had relocated again, from New Jersey to Massachusetts (a hotbed of early eventing activity). I was married and my wife May—also a rider—and I both worked at the Stoneleigh-Burnham School in Greenfield. But we wanted to live on a horse farm, in a place where we could spend more time riding and competing. We saw a farm advertised in Strafford, Vermont, and bought the place in November 1969. We moved there in June 1970 and have lived there since.

We picked this location to be in the middle of an active eventing area. Our farm is about three miles from Huntington Farm, where our friends Essie and Read Perkins lived at that time. It's seventeen miles from Dartmouth College, twelve miles from Hitching Post Farm, twenty-seven miles from the Green Mountain Horse Association—my "home away from home" for many years—and about an hour north of the farm in South Reading, Vermont, where my parents lived until 1985.

Vermont real estate back then was affordable, there were miles of dirt roads and trails for riding, it was an area that was very familiar, and as I've already mentioned, it was in the heart of New England horse country. It was the logical, almost inevitable move for us.

I started my own real estate agency, so that I would have more control over my daily schedule. This is just one example of the way that many riders manage to scramble and juggle their jobs with their riding time. For years, while teaching school, and (later) working in real estate, I kept my horse at barns with indoor rings so that I could ride after dark, even in midwinter.

Having Children: A Female Rider's Toughest Choice

It's statistically true that about 85 percent of eventing riders are female, so I am going to address some thoughts to those riders in particular. For years at our farm there has been an ongoing joke among the working students. "Wanted: Rich guy who loves horses and wants to support horse-crazy girl in her quest for Olympic fame." I don't think there are too many of those guys around!

There's a familiar scenario in which your boyfriend acts supportive during the courtship process, goes with you to events, and may even hold your horse while you walk the cross-country course. After you marry him, though, he increasingly whines and complains about how much time and money horses require.

Luckily, such a scenario, although common enough, is by no means universal. Lots of non-horsey husbands and wives trail along in a supportive role for years, and stay remarkably cheerful about it (most of the time).

Children require lots of time and money, both of which make it tougher for young mothers to pursue riding excellence. Among the unfair facts of "life circumstances" that I mentioned at the beginning of this chapter is that having children almost invariably impacts the mother's time more than the father's, although both share the financial obligations. It's usually easier for a riding father to leave the kids with the mother while he heads off for a weekend's competition than it is the other way around.

If a woman opts not to have children so that they don't interfere with her riding career, she may pay a psychological or emotional price in her later years. While many of her friends' lives are increasingly centered around their children and grandchildren, she won't have that circle of support. She may then wonder if the choice she made was too high a price to have paid. If she does decide to have children, she will have to juggle time and money in order to ride and compete. If money isn't a problem, then paid caregivers can look after the children; if funds are tight, however, something has to give. Very often that "something" is time on a horse's back, especially when children are little.

It might seem fundamentally unfair that this dilemma impacts women far more than it does men—but remember, "fair" doesn't exist in nature. A woman does have choices; it's just that these particular choices may be the toughest she'll ever have to make.

In the musical *Damn Yankees,* a middle-aged man named Joe Boyd sells his soul to the devil in order to be transformed into a baseball slugger who can help the floundering Washington Senators beat the arrogant New York Yankees. The musical has been called a retelling of the Faust legend, in which Faust, the protagonist of a German legend, trades his soul for diabolical favors. The term "Faustian Bargain" has devolved from that legendary exchange, and it strikes me that women who are desperate to ride may find themselves similarly tempted.

It's a biological fact that during a woman's twenties and thirties she may be at the apex of her skills as a rider. It's also true that those are the very same years when most women who want to have babies are most able to have them.

A woman who dreams of having a life with a husband and kids but who also enjoys the narcotic thrill of "big league" competition may be led to make that Faustian pact: "One more Olympic cycle, one more Quarter

Horse Congress. Then I'll have kids." And the "then" never happens.

There are hundreds of examples of women in riding who traded the dream of a "normal" family for the equally powerful dream of horseback riding prowess and glory. There are also many examples of women who were able to "have it all," a very supportive husband, and children, and a stellar riding career. So "riding versus family" doesn't necessarily need to be a choice, but stark reality suggests that very often it does become one.

"No Man Is an Island"

Build Your Support Network

You're probably a strong, independent kind of person, but when it comes to an undertaking as big and complicated as getting to be a good rider, being alone is a solitary journey you don't want to go on. I've known very few people in the world of horses who were true classic "loners." Almost everyone has at least some sort of support network, and for most of the very high-level riders, this network is broad, strong, and far-reaching.

Here's a scenario I've encountered over and over during my career: A twenty-something woman is devoted to her sport, but her husband or significant other is negative about her riding, the horses, and all the time and money she spends on this passion. Does this sound too close to home to be comfortable? If you and your riding aspirations are in a similar situation, you need to find a way to get your partner a bit more on your side. And whatever your environment at home, you need a support network that affirms and contributes to your efforts in a wide variety of ways.

Here's a great example from contemporary culture of one type of support network: I recently watched the 2005 film *The Sisterhood of the Traveling Pants* (based on the novel by Ann Brashares), the story of four teenage girlfriends who find a pair of thrift-shop jeans that magically fit them all. When they spend the summer far apart, they send the jeans from one friend to another at times of trouble; whichever friend is wearing the pants experiences the help and emotional support of her distant buddies. It's a web of mutual assistance that most of us would wish for at some time.

Another way to visualize a support network is to think of a stone dropping into a still pond, and watching the ripples spread out from the center. You are the center, and all those rings are your sources of support. The very nearest rings are the people whose influence you find the most crucial. This might be your husband or wife, parents or family, your closest friends, your sponsor or your riding teacher. Out there in the farther ripples might be your hay dealer, the mechanic who keeps your truck and trailer on the road—fairly distant, but still part of the overall equation.

For this network to be strong, the crucial people in the "inner circle" have to understand your passion at least a little bit, so that they are more likely to uphold and uplift you than drag you down. The problem with any passion is that the people who don't share the passion often "don't get it." It's easy to see how this can be so.

Many of the people I know around our winter base in Southern Pines, North Carolina, which is next door to the golf "mecca" of Pinehurst, are total golf fanatics. Every time I go into a local restaurant, I see tables full of golfers, all talking exuberantly about their round that day. Just as we equestrians bubble over with horse jargon, golfers talk about drives, slices, hooks, and lots of other terms I barely comprehend. I neither like nor dislike golf; I'm basically indifferent to it. When I'm on the receiving end of one of these conversations I nod, smile, utter little niceties—"uh huh, uh huh"—but I don't really "get" it, and I don't really have any interest. So I can see how easy it would be to totally bore someone with talk of my riding or my horse. ("Uh huh, uh huh. Denny, that's nice …")

■ Make Allies of Your Family

If the person I'm boring to death with my constant horse chatter is a very close family member, especially a husband, wife, or child—someone whose support I really need in order to improve my riding, or further my riding career—then I must find a better way to explain how I feel. If I can't explain myself, I'm not likely to create an ally in my quest. Just as I don't "get" a passion for golf, most non-horse people don't "get" a passion for horses. I don't think the key is to try to "convert" our key potential allies to horse lovers, but I do think we have to somehow make them understand that the passion is real, deeply meaningful, and sincere. This is often an extremely delicate negotiation, on the order of the Israeli-Palestinian Peace Process, because the ones with whom we're most often forced to negotiate are already negative about the time and money our horse activities drain from the family. (Henry Kissinger, George Mitchell, or some other accomplished diplomat needs to write a paper: "How to negotiate with your family about your horse so that both sides can win.")

"Mom, all you do is ride that dumb horse."

"Cindy, I just opened the vet bill. It's over three hundred dollars, and I don't think that's the last bill we're going to get."

"Why can't you get rid of that damn horse?"

The problem is that you know, and I know, and they know, that the complaints are absolutely justified. Your son would far rather you come watch his Little League game than ride "that dumb horse." Your husband really would rather not have to pay out more money to sustain "that damn horse." In many ways they will never truly understand how your moments of freedom and exhilaration on "that dumb horse" are the most crucial times in your week, providing a sense of joy and release from stress. Something has to give, and huge numbers of horse lovers find their life is a gigantic juggling act, which may cause more stress and strain than they can endure. Often it's the horse that has to go.

Yet many people do manage to keep their family happy, and to ride. These are the people who have somehow convinced their family that the need to ride and be around horses is an intrinsic piece of their soul—and that when their soul is fulfilled, they are a better spouse and better parent.

It was very fortunate for me that my wife, May, didn't need to be sold on "the horse thing," because she was just as hooked on horses as I was (fig. 7). May has been my sort of "one-man-band" network all these years—always supportive, but more of a realist than I, less of a dreamer, and much more likely to see what's really there, rather than trying to see what it would be nice to see.

Fig. 7 In horse sports, it seems that there are three basic ways spouses or significant others can respond to another's passion for horses and for riding. They can be actively supportive—the best case scenario. They can be mildly indifferent, the case of "you do your thing, and I'll do mine." Or, worst case scenario, they can be critical and negative, especially about the amount of time and money that horses require. I was lucky that May's interest in horses was at least as great as mine, so that she was incredibly supportive. Here, May is riding Opera Ghost at the Longleaf Pine Horse Trials in North Carolina.

If your life isn't to be one never-ending firestorm of bickering with your family or significant other, then he/she/they are the first people you have to enlist in your support network. The next ripple in the series of concentric circles I mentioned would be your close friends. Then, working out from that center…

Widen Your Network

▉ Riding Teachers

These are key choices. For many riders, teachers are the individuals who will have the greatest impact on their future success or failure. I say "teachers," plural, because most riders have a succession of teachers, just as we have a succession of teachers as we go through the grades at school and college. It's not uncommon in some riding disciplines, like eventing, for a rider to have one teacher for dressage, another for jumping, and perhaps even a third for cross-country.

Teachers are also called coaches or trainers, and there may be subtle differences among these roles, but essentially all of them have knowledge that you need to acquire, and their job is to impart that knowledge to you.

I once read that a totally motivated student could learn as much from a public library as from Harvard. And while it's true that the sum total of accumulated thought might be encapsulated in a great library, the problem is that most of us don't learn as well "passively" as "actively." We need what a Harvard has, and a library lacks: great teachers who inspire and invigorate us to learn.

It's quite well established that different individuals absorb information in different ways. In sports, the transfer of information usually occurs in three main ways, and while all three are important, we each grasp new concepts, or solidify old ones, in our own sequence of the three.

Visual Learning

The first method is basically "Monkey see, monkey do." The instructor, or other accomplished rider, demonstrates a movement or technique, and the student tries to copy it.

Auditory Learning

In the second method, the instructor very carefully explains what each body part is meant to do in, for example, picking up the right lead canter.

Kinesthetic Learning

The third method might be dubbed the "shut up and ride" method. The student drills and drills to absorb what the movement feels like.

If a student is primarily a "shut-up-and-ride" learner, and if the instructor interrupts the flow of work every few minutes to give a detailed explanation, then the student's learning process gets constantly disrupted. On the other hand, if the student craves explicit directions, but is told to "shut up and ride," then she isn't getting what she needs from that particular teaching style.

Known for her bold style and "go for it" mentality, Dani has numerous Grand Prix wins to her name, including the $384,000 Rolex Grand Prix CSI5* Winter Equestrian Festival in Wellington, Florida, in 2018, and the 2019 $391,000 Rolex Grand Prix CSI5* and Longines Global Champions Tour—Shanghai.

Danielle Waldman and Lizziemary at the World Equestrian Games in Tryon, North Carolina, in 2018.

Discipline: Show Jumping

Dani has competed on all the major stages in the sport, including top finishes at the 2018 World Equestrian Games, the 2015 and 2017 European Championships, and the 2017 and 2018 Global Champions Tour. In 2010, Dani acquired Israeli citizenship and has been competing for the country ever since. At the World Equestrian Games in Tryon, North Carolina, she led a historic first-ever Show Jumping Team for Israel.

Life circumstances:

I was born and raised in New York City to Jewish parents who had no history in the horse world. My father was number one in the world in squash, and my mother was a nationally ranked squash and tennis player, so I grew up in a very competitive sports family. I played competitive tennis as a kid, but as I got more into horses, I stopped with the tennis and focused entirely on riding.

Hooked on horses when:

I got into horses by chance through a schoolmate who asked if I'd like to go riding one day—I loved animals and was a bit of a "country mouse"…and I was hooked immediately.

I think I got good because:

↪ The main reason I feel I have found success is because I refuse to let the bad moments get me down. I always fight and try to look forward and not backward.

↪ I am mentally tough: I don't get nervous and actually excel with pressure.

↪ I also got good because I was lucky enough to be given many opportunities to work with top professionals and ride top horses. When I came back to the sport after taking time off for college, I needed to sit on as many horses as possible.

↪ I've always struggled with authority, and I rode by myself for a long time, but now I value having someone on the ground.

My most important advice:

Look where you're going, not where you don't want to go!

Danielle G. Waldman (Dani Goldstein)

If the instructor or one of her better students cannot or will not demonstrate how something should be done, then the very powerful "watch-and-copy" style of visual learning isn't available.

Different teachers not only have different teaching methods, they also have different styles. Some are gentle, caring, and supportive, while others shout, criticize, and bellow like Marine Corps drill sergeants, and there are all varieties between these extremes.

Then, of course, there is an enormous range of sheer competence among instructors. Returning to the Harvard example, one of the obvious features of the world's great universities is that the school has retained the most brilliant and accomplished scholars and teachers on its faculty. I have no doubt that at various obscure community colleges there are teachers as gifted as those anywhere, but such individuals would be the norm at Oxford, Harvard, and Stanford, for example.

There are great riding instructors who are gifted and innovative teachers, the kind of teachers who train the best riders in the world. Then there are other instructors who simply don't know much, and teach the little they do know very poorly. Even more dangerous are instructors who actually teach *incorrect* information. I suppose "correct" is subject to interpretation and opinion, but some situations are never correct. First among these is sheer horse abuse. Unfortunately, some so-called trainers and teachers constantly resort to painful and coercive methods to force scared horses to perform actions that the horses haven't been properly prepared to achieve.

If you go to the stables of the great horsemen and horsewomen in the world, and I mean even "out behind the barn," out of sight of the public, you will see quiet, humane, systematic work. Yes, there will be brief episodes of strong reinforcement every so often, but the constant overall tone will be harmonious teaching rather than coercion.

You will never, ever see a horse with his head tied around to his stirrups to "supple him on his left side." Draw reins, if used at all, will be for subtle reinforcement of correct aids, not as a means of forcing a horse into a painful shape. You won't see lots of whipping and spurring, nor will you see harsh yanks on the horse's mouth by hard, uneducated hands. You won't see frantic, lathered horses living in a constant nightmare of force and pain and fear, and you won't hear lots of harsh yelling

A Tale of Two Coaches—
Polar Opposites

My own riding has been influenced most strongly by Jack Le Goff (see p. 52) and Walter Christensen, two brilliant horsemen who were polar opposites of one another in terms of their personalities and teaching styles.

Jack loved the glare of the spotlight. He reminded me of that old quotation, "He wanted to be the bride at every wedding and the corpse at every funeral." He was loud, bombastic, theatrical, bullying, and cajoling, one of those people who light up a room with the bright flame of their personality (fig. 8).

Jack could tear you down one moment, and the very next he could convince you to go conquer the world, so deftly could he read your psychological makeup. He was a Frenchman to the core of his being, the essence of a "bon vivant."

Walter Christensen was calm, measured, thoughtful, analytical, and quiet (fig. 9). He was the prototype of the systematic German; not the barking, scary German of the old World War II movies, but the kindly sort of German who might have sat in a little shop meticulously making wooden toys for children.

Walter could soothe a nervous horse merely by entering his stall. I once watched him take the electric clippers from a young apprentice, and proceed to clip the bridle path of a horse that had been rearing and trembling just moments earlier.

I remember each of these men vividly, but in very different ways. Perhaps I needed what each had to tell me, in the way he knew how to tell it, at two quite different stages of my riding life.

Fig. 8 Jack Le Goff seemed to live his life at a burning level of intensity, and you had to be careful not to be singed by the flame. Jimmy Wofford said that Jack didn't care if he "broke your egg to make his omelet." He was a great coach, but a hard-pushing and aggressive one, and you had to be able "to stand the heat or get out of the kitchen" if you wanted to ride for the USET during his winning era.

Fig. 9 Because eventing is comprised of disparate "pieces," it's common for event riders to seek help from specialists in the disciplines of show jumping and dressage. Here, in the early 1980s, I'm riding York at a New England Dressage Association clinic with the German trainer Walter Christensen, coach of the Swedish bronze medal dressage team at the 1984 Olympics in Los Angeles. Acting as his interpreter is Louise Natthorst, who would become a member of that Swedish team.

A Coaching Vignette

Sometimes there are coaches so gifted at manipulating the hearts and minds of their players that they transcend ordinary coaching to become legendary figures in their chosen sports.

In my lifetime there have been three of these coaches connected with the United States Equestrian Team: Bertalan de Nemethy and George Morris, both coaches of the USET Show Jumping Team, and Jack Le Goff, who arrived in the United States from his native France in 1970, hired to revive the flagging fortunes of US Eventing.

In July 1974, the US Eventing Squad chosen to compete at the Burghley World Championship Three-Day Event in September flew from New York to London to spend a couple of months leading up to the big event training at a facility in the south of England.

We were, as Stalin said to the Russian troops as they finally invaded German soil, "in the belly of the beast." Through the late 1960s and well into the 1970s, the English Three-Day Team had crushed all opposition. As we began our tentative challenge to that English might, we were painfully aware that our English hosts were the reigning gold medalists from both the 1970 World Championships and the 1972 Olympic Games.

One quiet summer evening a wave of excitement swept the American camp. Richard Meade, the captain of the English team and the current Olympic goal medalist, was coming to try a horse that someone had brought in as a sales prospect.

All six of us trooped down to the show-jumping arena to watch Richard school this horse, and we were perched on the top rail like six birds on a wire. I looked down the country lane that passed by the schooling area, and who should be strolling toward us but our coach, Jack Le Goff, complete with fishing rod, reel, and high-topped waders.

I was sitting next to our team captain Mike Plumb, and I said something to him like, "Won't Jack be interested to watch this?"

Mike replied, "He won't even stop." Sure enough, Jack walked right on by, smiled, called out, "Hello everybody. Hello Richard," but didn't even pause.

Mike knew Jack better than I did, and he also understood Jack's psychological insight into his riders. Later, I also understood what Jack had done, but I didn't at the time.

Jack wasn't going to validate Richard Meade in our minds by paying him the slightest attention. To acknowledge that this gold-medal winner had anything to show that was worth Jack's time would not have been the way to persuade us that we had what it took to beat the world's predominant three-day-event team.

Thirty-four years later I told this story to George Morris, another Olympic gold medal coach. "Jack is a genius," said George, "and you know I don't say that about many people."

and swearing. If your instructor routinely employs such methods, your best choice is to run, not walk, to the nearest exit—even if that instructor is winning everything in sight.

The instructor you choose, probably more than any other person, will influence much of your attitude toward riding and training. When your instructor is quiet, systematic, patient, and thorough, those qualities will "rub off" on you. When an instructor is harsh, rough, and overly demanding, his students will be more likely to interact with horses in a coercive manner.

You aren't locked into any particular teacher, even though some teachers try to create "disciples" rather than students. You may be the kind of person who feels secure and comfortable in a "master-disciple" almost cult-like relationship, or you may be a "ping-pong ball," constantly bouncing from one instructor to another in the endless quest for the magic answer. You have to find the instructor-student equation that works for you, and the right choice or choices in this relationship, probably above all others, can determine how far you will be able to rise.

Note that when I say "the instructor-student equation that works for you," that phrase is open to broad interpretation! What "works for you" may not be the teaching approach that helps or makes you become the best possible rider, but rather the one that keeps you happily and safely in your comfort zone.

This is possible because you *hire* the coach. If you don't "like" him or her for some reason, you can fire your current coach and hire a different one. By contrast, if you were on a high school, college, or professional sports team, you would be *assigned* a coach—period, end of statement. If you didn't like that coach, your choices would be simple: Deal with it, or quit the team.

In 1974, I was selected for the squad of nine riders who trained at the USET Three-Day Team headquarters in South Hamilton, Massachusetts, to determine which six would represent the United States at the World Championships the following September. The coach of the team was the recently hired former French Olympic rider, Jack Le Goff.

Jack (who passed away in 2009) was many things, but "warm and fuzzy" wasn't one of them. He could be tough, loud, tyrannical, insulting, and bombastic, and he didn't care one iota about "hurt feelings." What he did care about was winning.

If you happened to be grist for Jack's mill as I was, there were many times that, given the choice, like me you'd have traded for a "nicer" coach. Luckily for me, I had no choice, and later that fall I found myself being handed a gold medal by Prince Philip in Burghley, England, something that would never have happened if I'd traded Le Goff's insults and pressures for nurturing and praise from a lesser coach.

For more insight into the psychology of a winning coach, read *Instant Replay: The Green Bay Packers Diary of Jerry Kramer*. Kramer's coach was the legendary Vince Lombardi—like Le Goff, a man who knew how to create winning teams. Also, like Le Goff, Lombardi was not too worried if he "broke your egg to make his omelet." His players didn't love him, but he got them Super Bowl rings.

But you may want to love your coach, even though you're allowed to coast along performing at three-quarters of your real ability. That's a seductive trap from which to escape.

Think of the difference in former days between arranged marriages and those that sprang from romantic love. Parents who thrust their children into arranged marriages were concerned with mundane goals: economic prosperity, the production of healthy and competent heirs, and consolidating or stabilizing real estate ownership. These are hardly the objectives to make the new partners swoon with passion, but they were solid ingredients for other successful conclusions.

Perhaps your choice of a coach should be an arranged marriage, even if the choice doesn't make your heart beat faster. Is your objective a drumming heartbeat or horseback riding competence?

■ Mentor

Here's another key choice. The term "mentor" usually describes an older, experienced person who is supporting and guiding a younger, less experienced person along some path of endeavor. We usually think of this as unpaid advice and counsel, something the mentor does "out of the goodness of his heart." I recently read that the whole concept of mentoring is gaining renewed interest in business corporations, because a good mentor who has "been there, done that" can dramatically smooth the path for someone who might otherwise get on the wrong track.

There's a saying, "Experience is what you get a couple of minutes after you needed it." Trial and error, usually lots of error, is intrinsic to the learning process, but a good mentor who has already learned from his or her own errors can help you avoid experiencing the worst of these. I suppose that your mentor, if you have one, is the person you are most likely to go see, or call on the phone, when you're up against some problem and aren't sure how to fix it.

"Hi Barb, it's Sally. You know that new filly I bought last month? There's something sort of strange going on. Every time I ask her to.... What do you think?"

Or, "Hi Barb, it's Sally. I've got a chance to ride in the Linda Atkinson clinic in August, and I wondered what you think about that?"

And so on. The person to whom you feel most comfortable reaching out when you need advice, or help, or just encouragement, is your mentor. If you don't have such a person, you can seek one out. Think whose judgment you respect, and who you feel you might be comfortable with, and just go and ask for some advice about something. See how the person responds, and try to get a sense of whether the relationship can go anywhere. If it feels like a good match, see how it develops. If it doesn't feel right, approach someone else.

Sometimes the mentor finds you. Remember, there's something in it for that person, too, or the relationship could never be meaningful. Often, older people find their interest and eagerness rekindled by the energy and enthusiasm of someone younger and "upward bound." Your mentor will derive satisfaction and sheer fun from helping you reach your goals. You may, if you're lucky, have several people in mentor positions, but be careful not to make them jealous of one another!

Your teacher or your sponsor may also be your mentor, but sometimes their expectations of you are a bit judgmental or ego-related. They want you to do well under their instruction, or with their horse. A mentor's support, sort of like a mother's love, should just be there for you, on your worst days, as well as on your blue-ribbon days.

■ Barn Staff

These people are also known as "your horse's best friends." You may keep your horse(s) at your own place, but in an increasingly suburbanized world, more and more owners board their horses at stables owned and run by others. Whoever it is that manages the stable or farm where you board your horse, plus all the employees at the farm who actually take hands-on care of your horse—these are all people you want to have "in your camp." If you are an absentee horse owner, they are the ones who feed your horse, clean his stall, change his blankets, turn him out and bring him in, check him for injuries, and perhaps even groom him before you come to ride.

Do you take the time to get to know these key people in your horse's life? Do you know what they think he might need that he isn't getting? Do you solicit their advice? I've known some horse owners who treated "the help" with indifference and others who enlisted their support through warm and caring interaction, even though their social and financial worlds might be poles apart.

Again, common courtesy, common decency, and common good sense will make friends and allies whose support can be critical to your ultimate success, whereas cool disinterest will only actively ensure that the barn staff will never go out of their way to help you. Which path do you routinely choose?

■ Veterinarian and Farrier

There are two other individuals whose paid presence at your barn will probably be more frequent than you might prefer—your veterinarian and your farrier—sometimes both on the same day, and for the same reason! These two people are there to keep you on the road with a sound, healthy horse, and it all works better if they understand and support your goals. You may also use alternative therapy practitioners, such as chiropractors and massage therapists, and they should be considered part of this support network.

■ Breed, Discipline, and Other Associations

There are associations that primarily exist to promote (for example) the Morgan horse, or the sport of dressage. They are always "there for you" if you learn how to tap into their resources, and one of the very best ways to accomplish this is by getting to know (*personally* know) people at the organizational level.

Let's say you drive Morgans, and your goal is to represent the United States at the international level in singles driving. Now you automatically have three potential allies in your quest: the American Morgan Horse Association, the American Driving Society, and the United States Equestrian Federation, which has, as one of its departments, the High Performance division. Get online and do some research to find out "who's who" at those organizations, and go see them. They won't bite you! I realize that it sounds incredibly daunting, but usually the people that work for these big associations are exceptionally pleasant, helpful, and welcoming.

Or maybe you are working with a Quarter Horse in one of the many sports at which this versatile breed excels. Think about the American Quarter Horse Association, the world's largest equine breed registry and membership organization (more than 330,000 members in 2008). This vibrant organization, based in Amarillo, Texas, offers comprehensive programs for all ages, levels, and disciplines. If you ride a Quarter Horse— possibly the most popular and widely recognized breed in the United States—you are almost guaranteed to find some aspect of the AQHA that can help you in your quest.

Two more wonderful organizations that exist to weave a web of support specifically aimed at younger riders are 4-H and the US Pony Club. Once you join either (or both) of these associations, you have access to a broad array of educational and promotional opportunities, free instruction, and a built-in circle of like-minded and usually supportive friends.

Maybe you can do some volunteer work at a local level. Trust me, all associations are desperate for willing, positive volunteers, and it can be a wonderfully symbiotic relationship. You help the association, and at the same time you start to create a wider and wider network of contacts who can potentially help you.

Roxie is currently ranked the Number Two para dressage rider in the world. She competed on the US Para Dressage Team at the 2014 (Normandy, France) and 2018 (Tryon, North Carolina) World Equestrian Games.

Roxie Trunnell competing in Grade I Para Dressage on Dolton.

Disciplines: Para Dressage

Roxie was awarded the bronze medal at the 2018 WEG for her performance in the Grade I Musical Freestyle and was the individual rider for the United States at the 2016 Paralympics in Rio de Janeiro.

Life circumstances:

In 2009, my life was changed forever. One moment I was riding and enjoying life, the next I was in ICU on a ventilator, fighting for my very existence. A virus caused my brain to swell, then a tiny blood clot "rearranged my computer and navigation system." I was in a coma for three weeks, and upon waking up, I was unable to do any "coordinating movements," including speech. I endured endless hours of therapy, rehabilitation, and over the course of two years, I rode vaulting ponies, "little things" that didn't care if I wobbled or was unsteady. Eventually, I was allowed to walk and trot off a longe line. Then, on a cold day in December 2011, with the aid of several friends and family, I was able to sit on my girl, Touché, the horse I had ridden up to Prix St. George and had twelve years of competition experience on before my illness. The day I rode Touché gave me hope that I could ride a dressage test once more. I worked and worked and was classified as a Grade I Para Equestrian—that is the most disabled an equestrian can be. My official diagnosis of *Cerebellum Ataxia* causes tremors, fine motor issues, delayed response time, and issues with balance and coordination.

Hooked on horses when:

Ever since I could remember, horses have been a part of my life. I dreamed of horses, rode horses, and believed that my future would always contain a horse.

I think I got good because:

The main reason I became the rider I am today is because of my mare Touché. I have an incredibly special bond with her. She is a very spirited, red-headed mare and has put me in the dirt more times then I can count! After my illness, everybody was nervous to put me back on her but I was stubborn and wanted to ride her again. When she saw me sitting in the wheelchair, she bent her knees and leaned over to help make it easier to get me on her back. When I got off balance in the saddle, she would slow down or compensate and let me find my balance again. She recognized I was not the same rider I once was and made it her job to make sure I was safe. I ended up taking her to the 2014 WEG in Normandy, France, where she was the oldest horse there at eighteen-plus, but she showed those young horses how it was done! I made a promise to her there that I would never make her go down another centerline again if she just got me through my first big international show, and she did me so proud. I still ride Touché even though it's at a painfully slow walk or slow jog (she's twenty-five) but I will never ever sell her because she has done so much for me. Touché knew me before I got sick, and she now knows me like this, and she can accept the changes…so then the rest of the world can accept it as well.

↪ I have a very strong bond with Dolton (my competition horse), and when I am at a show, you can usually find me just hanging out with him at his stall. I'm sure there are people out there who think I am crazy for doing it, but there is some logic to my madness. I think that if you treat your horses like they're special, they will go out of their way to take care of you and give it their all in the show ring. Because when it comes down to it, it is just you and your horse out there in that ring. The extra time you spend with your horse matters and can be the difference between winning and losing.

↪ Another reason I think I am the rider I am today is that I don't get sucked into the political/gossipy side of international competition. Yes, I'm aware of my peers but I don't let it influence what I am doing. I'm the goofy rider that's always cheering on the others even if I'm not having a good show personally.

My most important advice:

I think it's a big misconception that just because you have a handicap or a disability, judges take that into account in para competition. They don't. You might be a para equestrian with a dispensation certificate, but judges expect you to make your tests look just as good as the FEI "able-bodied" tests. Becoming a para equestrian requires work and dedication. If you do that, you can achieve great things!

When I am in a competition, I have a little motto that I chant to myself right before I go into the show ring that calms my nerves: "It's just one movement." This has saved me a few times in the ring. During the 2016 Paralympics I messed up during the entry halt, but I took a deep breath and recited my motto, and I went on to have a really good test. Just because you mess up on one movement doesn't mean your whole test has to go to hell.

Roxanne Trunnell

■ Horse Dealers

Pay attention to my number-one slogan, "You have to have a good horse!"

Let's look at this statistically, the way they do at sales-training seminars for, say, encyclopedia salesmen. If I'm going to make a living as a door-to-door salesman, I have to knock on a very large number of doors, because most of my calls will be rejects. If I knock on twenty doors, I might sell one set of encyclopedias. If I knock on two hundred, I might sell ten, and if I knock on two thousand, I might sell two hundred sets. It's a very small percentage of winners, so I have to have a big pool of prospects.

That's how it is in the quest to find the good horse, assuming you can't afford to buy the cream that has already risen to the top. If you only look at ten horses a year, what are your chances of discovering that special one compared to your chances if you look at several hundred a year? Not so good. So, how do you position yourself to even get a chance to look at large numbers of horses? One way is to develop a network of horse dealers with whom you keep in pretty close touch, so that when they "get a new load in from Nebraska," you are one of the first people there to pick over the load.

There are several levels of horse dealers, from the top professionals with the beautiful stables in the high-rent districts of Equine America, to the "gypsy dealer" with a rusty horse trailer who picks up a horse here and there from the racetrack, or from local sales and auctions. Potential stars can be found hiding at any of these levels, but the top professionals are more likely to spot the fact that the "diamond in the rough," is, in fact, a diamond.

A Rolodex of phone numbers, or some variant of that on your computer (if you are computer savvy) can be an enormously valuable tool if you know how to employ the tool and are enterprising enough to actually use it. Keep in touch with your contacts, if you want them to keep in touch with you!

Over the years I've watched riders who figured out how to work the system, and who created strong, vibrant networks of support. I've seen countless others slogging away in the trenches (read: mucking out stalls) year in and year out. The riders who know how to get help usually—not always, but usually—are able to reach their goals much more often than those who go it alone. "No man is an island," wrote John Donne in "Meditation XVII." Those words were true then, and they are true today. If you ignore that truth, if you don't build bridges that are out there just waiting to be built, you will struggle in solitude, and you will very likely fail in solitude.

The Sponsor Dilemma

■ Not All Horses Are Created Equal

As the ripples of your support network spread out from the center, the next key person on your list would be your sponsor—or maybe not.

Most riders don't have a sponsor. They depend entirely upon their own income, or their family income, to pay every horse-related expense. That's one of the biggest reasons for the huge disparity between the quality of the horses ridden by wealthy—or sponsored—riders and the horses ridden by everybody else.

Think of the basic items of equipment that athletes bring to the arena in almost every sport other than riding, except maybe car racing and yachting. In most sports, all the players can afford equal equipment. We wouldn't expect one baseball player to use a real Louisville Slugger, and another to swing a broomstick. We wouldn't expect Tiger Woods to have the best clubs available, but V.J. Singh to have a set of rusty old vintage 1930 clubs.

When equipment is equal, the "edge" is just you, your skills, your guts, and your abilities, not the equipment you can afford. But in riding, the key item of "equipment" is your horse. If you ride some poor old fellow with the athletic skills of a plow horse, and your opponent is sitting on Secretariat, who is likely to win? It doesn't take a genius to figure that one out. That's why we see that so many of the world's top riders either come from rich families, or have managed to attract rich sponsors.

The harsh reality for the small percentage of competitors whose goal is the very top is that modern horse prices have put elite horses out of the financial reach of all but those with equally elite wallets. The top horses in many horse sports are selling, in the early years of the twenty-first century, for hundreds of thousands, even millions, of dollars.

Horses aren't the entire story. A new dual-wheel pickup truck and a four-horse gooseneck trailer will push $100,000. That's before you include diesel fuel, entry fees, saddles and equipment, travel and lodging, lessons and coaching—the myriad of expensive "pieces" that keep riders on the competition trail. Unless these riders either win the New York State Lottery (highly recommended), or as Donald Trump says about trust-fund recipients, "are members of the lucky sperm club," who is going to pay these bills?

There are always more aspiring riders than there are sponsors to support them, which leads to a classic catch-22 situation.

"I need good horses in order to win the success that will attract a sponsor. But I need a sponsor to buy me the good horses that will enable me to win."

At this moment there are probably at least twenty-five event riders in their twenties and thirties who are very good riders, indeed who are on the verge of "making it" to the big leagues. I'd guess that the same situation prevails in most of the other horse sports. But to return to my baseball-bat analogy, most of these riders step up to the plate at each competition, not with a Louisville Slugger, but with some variant of a broomstick. Or, if they do get their hands on a Louisville Slugger and begin to hit home runs, as soon as that elite horse vanishes (and horses vanish for a hundred reasons), they can't afford another. The home runs cease, and the rider falls back into the pool of struggling aspirants.

Read my lips: "You have to have a good horse." I'll say it again. A good rider on an untalented horse is about as effective as an America's Cup skipper sitting in a leaky rowboat. *You have to have a good horse* (fig. 10).

That's why, of my twenty-five hypothetical "famous riders in waiting," at least twenty of them will still be waiting ten years from now. They won't have figured out the magic answer to sponsorship that Jim Wolf, USET Director of Executive Sport Programs, phrased so perfectly: "You have to sell someone else on *your* dream."

■ Wooing the Sponsor: Come Fly with Me

The entity most likely to back your dream isn't some huge multinational company like Nike or Budweiser. It's much more likely to be a somewhat

Nobody Did It Better:
Frank Boyden of Deerfield Academy

Mr. Boyden, as I knew him in the 1950s and 1960s, lived about ten miles south of me in Deerfield, Massachusetts. He was a legendary figure in the independent school world, the last in a line of headmasters who had single-handedly transformed their schools into institutions of national significance. It wasn't until the publishing of John McPhee's *The Headmaster* in 1966 that I obtained a broader insight into how some of that was accomplished. Boyden's "secrets" apply with equal power whether you are soliciting allies in your quest to build a school or to support your horseback riding career, because these so called "secrets" are simply ways of getting people to think well of you and to want you to succeed.

Mr. Boyden wrote letters to thousands of people. Sometimes he'd write seventy a day. It's estimated that in his lifetime he wrote half a million letters. Once, when I'd had a particularly good academic semester at Dartmouth, there was a tiny, one-line clip in the Greenfield Recorder Gazette, the local paper for Greenfield and Deerfield: "Emerson Earns Highest Honors at Dartmouth." Several days later, there in my mail box in Hanover was a congratulatory letter from Mr. Boyden. I didn't know I was one of half a million, so I felt enormously flattered!

He drove around to church suppers and bake sales in the surrounding communities, just to introduce himself and make friends and allies for Deerfield Academy. He invited the local residents to watch Deerfield athletic events and the annual Gilbert and Sullivan operetta. He reached out in a thousand ways.

Once, when my father asked Mr. Boyden how he'd transformed a one-room school with twelve students that was about to close into one of the most prestigious preparatory schools in the world, he modestly answered, "Well, you see, Ed, I just kept everlastingly at it."

This low-key statement has always reminded me of President Calvin Coolidge's famous quote: "Nothing in the world can take the place of persistence. Talent will not; nothing is more common than unsuccessful men with talent. Genius will not; unrewarded genius is almost a proverb. Education will not; the world is full of educated derelicts. Persistence and determination alone are omnipotent. The slogan, 'press on' has solved, and always will solve, the problems of the human race."

Daryl won the CIC** at the Virginia Horse Trials with Rosie's Girl, an off-track Thoroughbred, in May of 2018.

Daryl Kinney brought Rosie's Girl along, from right off the track, all the way through the eventing levels, to eventual success at Advanced.

Discipline: Eventing

Upon graduating from college, Daryl started working for me. She stayed for over 10 years, starting many young horses and bringing them up the levels of eventing. I gave her the ride on Union Station after he had completed a couple of Preliminary

Level events. Union was an off-track Thoroughbred and quite a tough ride, but Daryl rode him in their first Intermediate, and eventually Advanced Level events. The skills she learned on Union allowed her to bring Rosie's Girl, another OTTB, along—from green and just-off-the-track, to success at the Advanced Level.

Life circumstances:
My mom had horses when she was growing up, so she was very willing to allow me to take riding lessons.

Hooked on horses when:
I started working at a local farm, and eventually I was there every spare moment.

I think I got good because:
- I never felt like I was overly talented, but I was always a hard worker. If I wanted to ride more I had to work for it, and I lived and breathed for horses. So, it was a no-brainer for me: work hard and you get to do what you love. I was fortunate to work for people along the way who recognized this and always helped me as much as I helped them.

- I have always enjoyed riding with one person and learning everything I could from that person. I wasn't one to bounce around from instructor to instructor looking for one to tell me what I wanted to hear. I wanted to ride with people who would push me to get better, and teach me how to ride and be a trainer. I left my riding instructor from high school to go to college, I left my college instructor when I graduated, then I went on to work for Denny Emerson for over 10 years. I feel like I really learned a system to train horses and riders. With his guidance I took two horses to Advanced, one of which had never competed before.

- I think always, always, *always* putting the horse first has helped me get where I am today. I have never been a person to rush my horse's training, and if I feel something isn't quite right, I never feel like I have to work the horse anyway. A healthy, happy horse is much more able to do the job you are asking of him and will stay sound and able to do the job a lot longer.

My most important advice:
Never give up. It sounds so cliché, but it is really the truth. In any equestrian sport there will be unbelievable highs and some terrible lows. It's just part of life. Horses tend to evoke such strong emotions from us, and when we eat, sleep, and breathe for them, it seems to make the lows lower. In truth, there is no guarantee you'll get as good as you want to, but you have no chance at all if you just quit. So keep plugging away.

Daryl Kinney

Fig. 10 It's hard to get on a "hot streak" with horses unless you get to ride good ones, as I did, thanks to the USET. Winning the Dauntsey Park event on the USET horse Irish Warrior (given to the USET by Patrick Butler) during the lead-up to the 1974 World Championships helped make me realize that I could beat English riders! Confidence builds on confidence, just as defeat can build on defeat.

older person who can't "go there" herself, but who has dreamed about horses (just like you) all her life, and is in a financial position to accompany you on a magic carpet ride as you take your shot at going there. But why should this sponsor choose *you*, you specifically, over any one of your twenty-four other equally keen and equally talented competitors?

You have to sell yourself. This is where "horse world meets real world." Just as any job aspirant has to impress the individual doing the hiring, so you, the rider, must impress your prospective "employer," your potential sponsor. I can't tell you how many riders just don't get it. They think that if they just keep training well and riding well, the sponsor will find them. They never read Dale Carnegie's classic work *How to Win Friends and Influence People*. They don't know how to win converts to their cause.

Riding well is a big part of the picture, perhaps the most important single part, but remember that all twenty-five "riders in waiting" can do that. What can *you* do, that the other riders don't do, that will make a sponsor want to go on *your* magic carpet ride instead of someone else's?

■ Horse Business vs. People Business

First, you need to grasp something that I heard Olympic gold-medal winner David O'Connor once say: "If I thought I was in the horse business, I'd never have made it. Instead, I realized that I was in the people business." David's widely recognized "people skills" helped him achieve the competitive pinnacle of his sport, then move to the leadership of the USEF.

Contrast David's attitude with this all too real scenario: Several years ago I was standing in the stable area of the Fair Hill International Three-Day Event. Three young women (maybe three of my twenty-five "in waiting") were animatedly chattering away about their respective cross-country rounds earlier that day. They were filled with the euphoria that follows the safe conclusion of a daunting mission, smiling and laughing and gesturing.

Earlier that weekend, Lana Wright, the event organizer, had introduced me to a slight, elderly lady who had been one of Fair Hill's long-time chief financial supporters. In other words, this woman, who now approached the group of riders, was one of the people most responsible for providing them with their chance that day to have done the very thing that had them brimming over with joyous laughter. Very pleasantly, the lady asked, "How did it go for you today, girls?"

There is a certain subtle body language in a group, which either opens to include a newcomer or subtly shifts inward to exclude. This woman got a brief flickering glance, a curt "It was good," and the group shifted inward to resume their discussion of the day. The older lady's smile faded, and she quietly walked away.

I watched this little scenario unfold, and I thought to myself, "How unkind, how rude, and how totally stupid."

There's a saying that as people get older they become increasingly "invisible and irrelevant" to young people, and I'd just seen this saying played out in action. Those three girls may have just had a successful foray into the horse business, but they were abject failures in the people business. Who would want to help *them*?

These three seemed not to have realized there are usually only three reasons why people support you. They are either related to you, by blood or by marriage; they are paid by you, like your vet and farrier; or *they like you and want to be around you*. It's really very simple. Do you act in ways that make people like you, and enjoy being with you, or is your personality such that you shut people out or drive them away as I'd just watched the three young competitors do? It's your choice.

There is also a fourth reason why people will want to sponsor you, but I'm always surprised at how few riders seem to grasp its importance. This is the public image that you convey, the "buzz" about you that is created by how you promote yourself and your services. Almost every business, large or small, uses some form of paid advertising, and also tries to elicit favorable—and, preferably, free—publicity. I have the sense that many riders don't think of themselves in business terms. They don't see their efforts to become better riders as mini-enterprises bound by the same business "rules" that govern the local bank, auto-repair shop, or grocery store.

People are more apt to patronize businesses (read: "support riders") that have a good image than those with either no image, or a poor image. You can create a positive image in a hundred ways. How do you dress? Neatly or "grunge"? Do you slouch, with a cigarette dangling from the corner of your mouth, fail to make eye contact, and mumble "Yeah," when someone asks you something?

If you're fortunate enough to excel at a competition, how do you respond to requests for interviews or a press conference? Appreciatively and cooperatively, or as if you're facing a firing squad? Is your barn neat and clean, or is it some version of "war-torn Europe?" Is your horse well turned out and shiny, is your tack clean, is your truck at least somewhat presentable? You'd better believe that all of these little details are things people notice.

Do you make an attempt to be positive and upbeat? At horse shows and gatherings, do you smile pleasantly, or look away, or scowl? Business owners, especially those whose businesses interact with the public, go crazy when their employees drive away customers because they can't, or won't, shed their negative attitudes. Employers *love* upbeat, positive employees. Do you somehow expect that you are immune from other people's judgment of you just because you are a good rider?

Two of the best American event riders, whose names I'm obviously going to keep private, have never gotten so much as a whiff of sponsorship because they are so miserable to be around. If they have a bad jumping round—knock down a couple of rails, for example—everyone runs for cover, even their few friends. They know that otherwise they are going to get their heads bitten off by these two Olympic riders, who probably wonder why lesser riders get sponsored, and they don't. Miss Charlotte Noland, famous former headmistress of Foxcroft School had a favorite saying: "Your altitude is determined by your attitude." Think about what that means, act accordingly, and doors hitherto shut will miraculously start to open.

And the List Goes on

Even as the ripples spread way out from the center of your network to hay dealers, feed suppliers, mechanics, and the contractors who repair the barn driveway, the friendly, courteous, and considerate manner that you bring to all these interactions will strengthen the support network you need to succeed.

Do you keep "everlastingly at" the process of getting and keeping allies, and building a strong support network to help you in your riding endeavors? That's what it takes.

Nine Character Traits of a Successful Rider

5

Who You Are

Our emotions, taken together with the way we *respond* to these emotions, create what is often called "character." It is *character* more than any other factor that determines the success or failure of your relationship with horses.

There are hundreds of possible character traits, of course; I've singled out nine key character elements to examine in detail, starting on page 76. Chances are, these nine are the parts of my own character that I had to work on the most as I made my way as a rider. I'm going to talk about:

- ◆ Patience
- ◆ Initiative
- ◆ Positive attitude
- ◆ Assertiveness
- ◆ Courage
- ◆ Work ethic
- ◆ Competitiveness
- ◆ Focus and detail orientation

Whoa! At this point you may be thinking that a dissertation on character is a long way from tips on how good riders get good, but believe me, it is like the best-kept secret of riding success. Why?

We horseback riders experience the same wide range of emotions as all other human athletes—but with a difference: We aren't alone. The horse we ride also has a wide range of emotions (and responses to them) *plus*, our emotions affect him and his emotions affect us. When a baseball player is nervous as he steps up to the plate, his baseball bat doesn't sense his anxiety and start shaking, too! But a horse can sense anxiety. As prey animals and creatures of flight, horses' basic atavistic response to stress is to "get outta Dodge."

Just as our individual reactions to our emotions create our unique character, so does each horse have his own character. Some are brave; some are timid; some are aggressive. And whatever *their* character, we can influence our horse most effectively if we have molded our own character to be like that found in good riders.

Character Is *Always* a Work in Progress

If we were unable to change the way we react to an emotion, all of us would still be stuck with our pre-nursery-school character. We would scream when we were hungry, scream when we were uncomfortable, scream when we were wet, and only hush when our basic needs were met. If we responded to our emotions at twenty, thirty, or forty as we did when we were three, we would be in an institution.

We know that as children grow, they constantly change their emotional response to life. Parents, teachers, peers, and others try to steer those responses into acceptable avenues. "Johnny, don't hit your little brother. Be nice to your grandmother. Study harder in school. Clean up your room."

At a certain age and stage in life, however, it's assumed that whoever Johnny is going to be, he's probably pretty much already there. If he is timid, impatient, nervous, or arrogant, that's who he is. The progress he made from infancy has presumably stopped at a certain plateau.

Wait a minute. If we accept this about ourselves, we are doomed as aspiring riders. This is where we do ourselves in: We assume that *who we are* is *who we have to be; that where we are* is *where we have to stay.* This assumption can be right or it can be wrong; it's up to us to *choose* which it will be.

Just as we can practice the sitting trot, so we can practice a character trait like courage. Although we may not change as quickly or as easily at thirty as we did at three, the potential for change is just as real as it ever was. But not if we don't think so!

The essence of improvement is change. Change from one state of being to another state of being can be painful and fraught with emotional and sometimes even physical peril. At the least, it drags you out of your comfort zone; that's why most people do hit a plateau and stay on it for life.

As long as there's life, there's hope for change. I believe that you absolutely have to accept this premise if you ever hope to become a better rider. Your emotional responses and character traits are just as subject to improvement as your mental and physical traits.

Suppose you know almost nothing about Prince Edward Island, except perhaps that it is in Canada, but you know that if you read up on Prince Edward Island for even one hour, you'll know more about it than you do now. That's *mental* improvement.

Or, say you have never shot at a target with a bow and arrow. You know that if you take some lessons, and shoot lots of arrows, you'll hit the target more than you would without the lessons and the practice. That's *physical* improvement.

Why, then, don't you believe that you can improve your character traits, which are such powerful factors in your riding achievement? You can. You can start to "practice" all the qualities important to your riding success (and which I'm about to explain). You can "practice" anything that you wish to change for the better. The trick is first to believe it is possible to change it, and then to figure out how to "practice" it.

Having said that, let's acknowledge that some of the innumerable variants of the emotions and personality traits that make you uniquely "you" are fairly susceptible to improvement, while others are as intransigent as the relationship between North and South Korea. Change what you can, and be smart about what you can't. There's only so much you

Jonathan gained international recognition when he and his horses were featured in a BlackBerry® commercial in 2011 and in a Red-Bull Media House Documentary in 2014. He was a Road to the Horse finalist in 2012 and 2014, being awarded the Jack Brainard Award for Horsemanship at his second appearance.

Jonathan Field jumping bareback and bridleless on Hal, who is featured in his book and became a Breyer® model horse in 2019.

Jonathan gained recognition early on for his breathtaking liberty performances. Here he is pictured with the horses featured in his book *The Art of Liberty Training for Horses*.

Discipline: Horseman & Clinician

A devoted teacher of horsemanship, Jonathan appears at clinics and equine expositions throughout North America every year. He and his horse Hal were special guests at Breyerfest at the Kentucky Horse Park in 2019, where Hal was commemorated with his own Breyer® model. Jonathan was invited to present at TEDx San Juan Island in June of 2019. He is also the author of the instructional book The Art of Liberty Training for Horses.

Life circumstances:

I showed both English and Western as a kid, then left school at an early age to follow my dream of being a cowboy and riding horses; I worked moving cattle on a half-million-acre ranch. Then I met Pat Parelli and ended up studying with him for 10 years. Another horseman named Ronnie Willis also had a big influence on the development of my horsemanship.

Hooked on horses when:

My mom was a dressage rider, and my dad was a working cowboy and a farrier, so horses were in my life from the beginning.

I think I got good because:

🐾 I was lucky as a young man to get to ride with, observe, and be taught the classical principles of dressage. Because my mom was a passionate horsewoman, she exposed me to great teachers and riders like Charles de Kunffy.

🐾 I found myself on the Quilchena Cattle Company ranch, living in a cow camp, and riding out at 3:00 a.m. to spend eight to ten hours a day in a saddle, six days a week, in rough, mountainous country. The working cowboy's job in this type of environment can only be done on horseback, and your life often depends on your horse to get you out of a tough spot, get you home late, and look after you when two bulls get to fighting and you need to get them apart! When I started riding that many miles in a day, I would leave camp, trotting out to the cattle, and I would be concerned about which diagonal I was posting on—I thought I was a "good rider." My first three ten-hour days were especially challenging: at the end of the day, my jeans were fused to my skin with a layer of blood. But over time I could feel my body change; I wasn't riding the top of my saddle anymore, I was riding my horse's body in time with his feet. The friction between the saddle and my seat stopped, and it began to feel really good in the saddle. And *that's* when all the great lessons I'd had from dressage teachers really fell into place.

🐾 It was a few years later that I met Pat Parelli and was inspired to ride a horse naturally. A new dream came into focus: I wanted to be able to walk out in a 50-acre pasture and mount my horse without a saddle or bridle and ride all over my ranch— over logs, down the trail, moving cows. I now wanted my horses to want to be with me as much as I wanted to be with them. My daily bareback rides took my riding to another level, and learning about the finer sensitivities and nature of the horse brought me closer to them than getting a job done or winning a ribbon.

My most important advice:

🐾 Find a great role model, coach, or mentor. Immerse yourself in every way you can, study hard, and be willing to do anything even just for the chance to observe. I worked for free, cleaned barns, and built fences…just so I could hang my head over that fence and watch my mentors work with horses.

🐾 I owe my success to the many opportunities that came my way, but most importantly, to the fact that I've always thought of myself as a student of the horse. I never forget to appreciate their brilliance—it inspires me to strive to learn more and be better.

Jonathan Field

Fig. 11 In 29 seasons of competing at the Advanced level of eventing, I had 14 horses at that level, about the equivalent of one every two years. Speed Axcel here, was my last. I rode her at Groton House in 1999 when I was 58, but that's not what I remember about her. She was so tense and nervous that I had to become a much more patient rider, or I simply "lost" her. It's never too late to change and improve character traits, something Axcel taught me after nearly 50 years of riding.

can do, realistically, in trying to become somebody different. This is as true of horses as it is of people. We learned it in kindergarten, on that little pegboard game. "Don't try to put the square peg in the round hole."

The Nine Key Character Elements

In chapter 1 I told you that it's hard to get really good if you're pursuing the riding sport that isn't right for you. Fortunately, there are so many horse sports that you can find one that dovetails with who you already are, so that you don't have to make titanic changes to find a good fit.

For instance, if you are neither an aggressive sort of person nor a big risk taker, and you find yourself "trapped" in a tough, risky sport like eventing, why would you continue? There are plenty of riding sports more ready-made for who you are. On the other hand, a wild and woolly, "only-happy-going-Mach-2-with-your-hair-on-fire" sort of rider will hardly find satisfaction endlessly perfecting walk, trot, halt transitions in dressage. A quiet, analytical, detail-oriented personality will be much happier *not* coming out of Chute Number 5 at the Cheyenne Frontier Days Rodeo, or pounding down toward the first fence at the Maryland Hunt Cup.

Whatever riding sport fits you best and whatever sport in which you're trying to excel, there are some elements of character that, if you consciously make them part of yourself, will help you succeed. *Don't underestimate the importance of this chapter.* You've probably heard it said that "Riding is 90 percent mental." I would amend that axiom to "…90 percent mental and emotional."

■ I. Patience—Avoiding those Meltdowns

If I were to choose a single trait that I could confer as a gift to struggling horse trainers all over the world, patience would be that trait (fig. 11). Here's why.

Webster's Dictionary defines patience as "the will or ability to wait without complaint…the bearing of suffering, provocation, delay, tedious-ness, etc. with calmness and self-control."

Let's consider the famous horseman's saying, "You have to build a horse like an onion, one tiny layer at a time." What is more tedious than this? What causes more delay than this? When a horse is physically and emotionally unready to "do what I want," and also lacks the knowledge of what "I want him to do," because neither I nor his previous trainers have taught him correctly, that horse will resist out of self-preservation.

We could easily feel that resistance as "provocation," a malign intent on the part of the horse. We can feel "suffering" as a result of the horse's resis-tance, aching arms from the horse pulling on us, physical jolts and slams as he veers, shies, and twists. All the words from Webster's definition that a patient person needs to bear: "suffering, provocation, delay, tediousness, etc." are all implicit in training, schooling, riding, and competing a horse.

Can you develop the ability not to lose emotional control under pressure? This may be the most important choice you will ever be asked to make, as someone who deals with horses. As an illustration, consider these three "variations on a theme of patience." Taken together, they constitute a type of "world view" about the training of horses and riders

Like Watching Grass Grow

According to a story I heard some years ago, an American dressage rider was taking a lesson with German Olympic dressage rider Gabrielle Grillo. The American had a tendency to become impatient with her horse's perceived lack of progress, leading to this (perhaps apocryphal) exchange:

Gabrielle Grillo: "Joan [not her real name], back in America, does your house have a lawn?"
Student: "Yes, sure, we have a lawn."
G.G.: "Do you have to mow the grass?"
Student: "Of course."
G.G.: "After you mow it, if you stand and stare, can you see the grass growing?"
Student: "No."
G.G.: "But in a couple of weeks, you have to cut the grass again, no? So when did the grass grow?"

Ms. Grillo's point, of course, is that progress is so slow and imperceptible that we are too close to see it on a day-to-day basis, often leading to the misconception that there isn't any progress.

The Plateau Concept

George Leonard's book, *Mastery,* is full of insights and his idea that learning isn't some nice upward progression really struck home with me. In his view, learning is a series of plateaus where progress may be happening, but, as in Gabrielle Grillo's grass-growing analogy, the process is too gradual to discern.

Most riders, most people, want progress. So often when I'm teaching a lesson, a rider asks, "Is this better?" They want improvement *now*.

But Leonard postulates that those on the true path to mastery have learned to accept seemingly endless plateaus of non-improvement, and have also learned to find satisfaction in practice for its own sake. They don't need constant reassurance that they are getting better.

People not on the path to mastery get sick of feeling stuck on these plateaus, so they conclude they aren't improving rapidly enough. They either pick a different sport, or perhaps a different instructor. Then, no doubt, the whole plateau scenario plays out once more.

I noticed this phenomenon years before I read about it in Leonard's book. Maybe there was a riding concept I had read in a book, or heard from some instructor, and I had at least a glimmering of *intellectual* understanding of the idea, but the accompanying feelings weren't there. Then one day, after weeks, months, even years of practice and struggle— *click-click!* The feelings suddenly locked into place, and I'd think, "So that's what Jack (or some other teacher) meant!" Something had been happening on that plateau, the grass had been growing, but only at that *click!* moment did I realize it.

The Dressage Training Scale (including Losgelassenheit)

Classical dressage riders adhere to a clearly delineated Training Scale of six elements in a definite, specific order. As this is not a how-to book, I only introduce this to amplify how the character traits of patience—or impatience—can enhance or impede the process of training the dressage horse (or any horse).

The Training Scale:
1 Rhythm
2 Suppleness
3 Contact
4 Impulsion
5 Straightness
6 Collection

Often incorporated somewhere within the first two elements of rhythm and suppleness is the German term *Losgelassenheit*, which can be

A 2008 team gold medalist at the Beijing Olympics with Cedric, Laura also earned a team silver medal at the 2006 World Equestrian Games (Aachen, Germany) with Miss Independent and a team gold at the 2018 WEG in Tryon, North Carolina, with Zeremonie.

Laura Kraut and Cedric in their second-place round in the Dublin Stakes, 2007.

The pair shine during the 2008 US Show Jumping Team Selection Trials for the 2008 Olympic Games.

Discipline: Show Jumping

In addition to riding on several winning US Nations Cup teams, Laura has been the individual winner of more than 100 major Grands Prix, both at home and abroad. She is an ambassador for Just World International, which funds education and nutrition programs for children in impoverished communities.

Life circumstances:

My mother, Carol Kent, was always involved with horses and loved them, so I was first on a pony at age two and entered my first lead-line class when I was barely three. My sister Mary Elizabeth, just sixteen months younger, followed suit.

Hooked on horses when:

I always really loved horses; my mother's most effective form of punishment was that if I misbehaved, I couldn't go to the barn.

I think I got good because:

👉 Riding jumpers was something I wanted from an early age, but I didn't have a lot of financial backing so I had to wait. During my junior career I groomed and braided, and didn't mind doing any of that; it was all a part of the whole. When I went to work for Roger and Judy Young after the juniors, I continued braiding a lot to make extra money—basically, just to be able to ride *anything*!

👉 My years in the hunters taught me a lot of finesse, how to quickly and smoothly get a horse to the jump in the best possible style. You have to sit quiet on the hunters and get them to respond just off "feeling," without taking a pull or giving a kick. I was nineteen before I sat on my first jumper, but that feel and fluidness gave me an advantage. I got a lot of catch rides on hot, sensitive horses when I first started my own business.

👉 Then, when Geoff Sutton asked me to ride his Thoroughbred/Quarter Horse jumper Simba Run (not a typical jumper), we just clicked, maybe because of everything I'd learned up to that point. We were team alternates for the Barcelona Olympics (1992) and represented the United States at the 1994 World Cup Finals.

👉 I've always been open-minded about getting pointers from anyone. I got a lot of good help along the way—from Emil Hendriks in Holland, from Nick Skelton and Katie Prudent (who was very instrumental in helping me get to Europe to show), and, of course, from George Morris.

My most important advice:

As I've gotten older I realize that *patience* is a very important quality in this sport. It's important not to get upset or frustrated when the things you wish for aren't happening right away. Getting to the top takes a lot of determination and hard work. That, plus patience, helps you to be ready when the other essential ingredient comes your way: a little bit of luck at the right time.

Laura Kraut

defined as "looseness" or "an absence of tightness." This quality is both physical and emotional, in that an emotionally tense, apprehensive horse cannot be expected to move in a relaxed, flowing manner.

As these elements of the Training Scale are sequential, it follows that the trainer must not proceed to Steps 3, 4, or 5 until the horse has mastered Steps 1 and 2, and is rhythmic, supple, and basically calm and unworried in the work. "Looseness" is more important in some sports than in others, but all sports require a progression in which the building blocks at the bottom must be in place before the horse can move on.

But what if the rider lacks patience? What if the rider doesn't think the grass is growing, or is sick of feeling stuck on the same plateau?

The trainer intellectually knows not to press a nervous horse and knows that staying with Steps 1 and 2 of the Scale until the horse is less anxious is the correct thing to do—"But, damn it, I need to get on with the job!"

So the trainer escalates the training process into an adversarial relationship, the horse gets more worried, the trainer gets more frustrated and angry, and the Training Scale has been breached. Because the situation is so difficult and frustrating for the rider, it's very easy for the rider to conclude that the horse is being "bad," and to feel justified in punishing the horse. This happens in real life every day, because the trainer lacks patience and wants quick results that the horse hasn't been correctly trained to give.

◼ II. Initiative: Do You *Make* Things Happen, or *Let* Them Happen?
Years ago, Simon Turner, a friend who is a veterinarian at Colorado State University, sent me a little desktop slogan. It read: "There are three kinds of people in the world. Those who make things happen, those who let things happen, and those who wonder, 'What happened?'"

You are at a distinct advantage if it is in your nature to take the initiative and make things happen instead of waiting around to see if anything good will fall out of the sky. My own "horse history" bears this out.

I may have made lots of mistakes in my nearly sixty years of involvement with horses, but I don't think lack of initiative was ever one of them. I was pretty young when I started to seize the initiative in my fledgling riding career. I didn't come from a family that had anything to do with horses. I would say that my parents' attitude toward my riding was quietly supportive, in that they paid for my first three or four horses, but they were busy with their own life and basically let me pursue my interests.

If I did well, they'd say, "That's nice," and if I didn't, they'd say, "That's too bad." Otherwise, their attitude toward my horse career was very much hands-off, basically "benign neglect." I was left to my own devices starting from when I began riding Paint, my creatively named pinto pony, at about age ten. (My parents bought him from Louis Goodyear's sales barn in Sunderland, Massachusetts; the $250 price included a "silver-mounted" Western saddle and bridle.)

I lived on the campus of Stoneleigh Prospect Hill School, in Greenfield, Massachusetts, where my parents were heads of the school. In 1955, I discovered in the school library a copy of the Green Mountain Horse Association Magazine containing an article about the 1954 100-Mile Trail Ride, held the previous fall at GMHA in South Woodstock, Vermont.

I decided I wanted to ride in the GMHA 100-mile ride the following summer of 1956. I was thirteen years old and had been showing in gymkhanas for just two years. I knew nothing about long-distance riding, conditioning, the rules of the sport—really not much other than that I wanted to do it.

So I wrote to GMHA, and in due course received a letter saying that I would be sent an entry form the following spring when they were printed. By this time I'd outgrown Paint, and sold him to a local family. I'd found another horse—a bright bay Quarter Horse gelding at Louis Goodyear's—and named him Bonfire, after a horse in a Walter Farley book.

Remember the old diaries I mentioned in chapter 3? The entries from 1956 show how my initiative included preparations toward my summer goal that began in the depths of Massachusetts winter:

January 2

I went riding in the morning. In the afternoon we measured the route to Bernardston. It is eleven miles round trip. (The measurement was to enable me to track my 100-mile preparation.)

Fig. 12 In 1955, I read about the Green Mountain Horse Association's 100-Mile Trail Ride in a GMHA magazine in the Stoneleigh Prospect Hill School library's magazine rack. Then and there, I decided to do the ride. I sent for an entry form, and armed solely with articles about the ride, conditioned my second horse, Bonfire, all summer of 1956. This is Bonfire being examined by Head Judge, General Wayne Kester, August 29, 1956, in front of the former Woodstock Inn Stables, Woodstock, Vermont. Eleven days earlier, I'd turned 15. Four days later, we completed the 100 miles.

February 11
I went riding for a while in the afternoon. (I was home for the weekend from Phillips Academy in Andover, where I was "away" at high school without my horse.)

March 16
I went riding in the morning and Bonfire went pretty good. (Spring vacation!)

March 18
I went riding this afternoon and for the first time used a saddle. He (Bonfire) is feeling pretty good these days so I have quite a lot of fun.

In the 1950s, I could ride through the Stoneleigh woods and head north on Swamp Road all the way to the Vermont border, about ten miles away. Today the campus is boxed in by Interstate 91 and Route 2. That spring and summer of 1956, I took longer and longer rides:

June 8

I got up early so I could go riding before it got too hot. I went up to Bernardston the short route, and Bonfire seemed quite fresh when I got back.

June 11

Jack and I rode down to Louie's [Louis Goodyear] this morning, and had lunch in Sunderland. We didn't ride back until it got cooler. I think it was a 14-mile ride.

August 14

Rode practically to Vermont with Jack. At least 30 miles.

Later in August, my parents borrowed a wooden, home-built, one-horse, open-topped, horse trailer, and hauled Bonfire and me to South Woodstock (fig. 12):

August 28

Arrived in Woodstock.

August 29

Horses judged in.

August 30

First day of ride.

August 31

Rained all day.

Despite the rain, less than two weeks after my fifteenth birthday I completed my first 100-mile competitive trail ride with Bonfire.

How did it happen? Because I had the initiative to make it happen. Much of my subsequent career with horses came about in pretty much the same way.

■ III. Positive Attitude: Do You Draw People to You, or Drive Them Away?

A positive attitude beats a negative attitude every single time. People

Self-Confidence and the "Flea Jar Factor"

Assertiveness is, in my experience, a facet of self-confidence. So it may be that the common lack of assertiveness in riders is closely related to a lack of self-confidence. Improving your self-confidence is a conundrum. People who are urged to be more self-confident will ask, and rightly so, "How can I have the confidence to be more self-confident if I lack confidence in the first place? Isn't this a catch-22?"

I think the answer is both "yes" and "no." I like the saying, "Boldness comes from confidence; confidence comes from success." So you

Fig. 13 Keep pushing your limits, whatever your sport may be. Make this a habit. As Jane Savoie says, "Build yourself a bigger flea jar." Core Buff only needed to jump three feet, eleven inches to compete at advanced level, but here he's stretching to five feet, so three feet, eleven inches won't seem so big. I'm building him a bigger flea jar!

have to begin by guaranteeing success. The way to guarantee success is to begin with tasks that are ridiculously easy and gradually build from there, backing up if things start to go wrong. It's like desensitizing your horse to that scary ditch.

There are three things you try not to do when teaching a horse a new skill. Don't hurt him. Don't scare him. Don't get him wildly excited. Similarly, if you are trying to build your self-confidence, don't hurt yourself, and don't scare yourself—too much. You have to scare yourself a *little* to give yourself something to build on, but only a little. Keep doing the slightly scary thing until you have had so much success that you know success is inevitable. Then make whatever it is that you are trying to do a little harder. And so on. (At some point, it will get too hard, no matter how talented you may be.)

You can be timid, or shy, or indecisive, or reticent. You can be burdened by any one of many afflictions that result from a lack of self-confidence, and you can improve every one of them if you can figure out a way to scare yourself just a little bit. Too big a scare, and you will find your self-confidence in pieces on the ground.

If you don't like public speaking, don't start by addressing the Republican National Convention! Instead, maybe you could start by addressing Cub Scout Pack Three, so that your listeners are nine years old. Ski down the bunny slope first, not the double black diamond.

Jane Savoie is an internationally accomplished dressage rider who has written motivational books and is in great demand as a speaker. One of her stories that I like best describes how, if you put fleas in a jar and screw a lid on it, the fleas will initially hit their tiny flea heads against the lid while attempting to jump out. Some sixth sense then tells them exactly how high the lid is, so that they keep jumping—but not quite high enough to hit the lid.

Now, when you take the lid off the jar, the fleas will keep jumping—and although they could easily do it, they won't jump high enough to jump out. They have it in their tiny flea brains that the height of their jar is their limit. "So," asks Jane, "aren't we like those fleas? Don't we all have limits that are only real because we believe them to be real, not because they are real in fact?"

I told that story to some Radnor Hunt Pony Clubbers I was teaching in a clinic one fall. When I returned the next year, a little boy came up to me and said, "Denny, I'm a lot better this year. I have a much bigger flea jar!"

You can build *yourself* a much bigger flea jar (fig. 13). At some point, it will be so high that you won't be able to jump out of it—you are, after all, only mortal—but it might be very high, much higher than it is today.

with negative attitudes spread gloom and misery like a contagion. These depressing people lurk in every office, every business, every sports team, every barn—everywhere, around the world, staining their surroundings with their unhappiness. It's usually not enough for them that *they* be miserable; their one ray of happiness comes from making everyone else unhappy.

Being miserable is a choice. Being upbeat, positive, and sunny is also a choice. Years of "being down" may even make being miserable seem so normal as to be beyond choice! It's a very hard state to change, but you can change it if you so choose.

The reason to try to change: When you are gloom and doom personified, people shun you, which makes you feel even more gloomy. You create your own misery in a widening spiral. You wallow in it, and you invite everyone around you to join you down in the cold mud. Do you wonder that you lack a cheering section of supporters?

Negative people usually don't get as far as upbeat, positive people, and why is that such a surprise?

How can you choose to change? Maybe you don't even realize that you are slouching around with a storm cloud over your head. But if everything seems wrong, and nothing seems right, do a "storm cloud check."

Ask the people who deal with you on a regular basis. They may be tiptoeing around you, trying so hard not to awaken your inner bear that they won't answer you honestly, at first. Look at yourself closely. Would *you* really enjoy being around *you*? If you wouldn't, isn't this a change that you'd like to make?

Negative thinking, a great depressor of self-confidence, is just as much a bad habit as looking down, or posting on the wrong diagonal.

■ IV. *Assertiveness*: Getting Your Own Way—Nicely!

Assertive people tend to get their own way rather than be pushed around by others; as riders, assertive people tend to get their own way rather than being pushed around or ignored by their horse.

Legendary USET coach Jack Le Goff, with his strong French accent, was known to shout "Don't be a passenger!" (or something that sounded like that) at riders he felt were being ineffectual and unassertive. To Jack, a *passenger* is a rider who lets it happen and takes what the horse doles out. A *rider* was someone who made it happen, imposing her will upon the horse to obtain the desired result.

Another "Jack-ism" along these lines: "I am galloping my horse down to the big oxer. I pick up the telephone to dial the horse. But there is no answer!"

When you are "galloping to the big oxer," you normally sit up a bit and, through the use of half-halts, ask your horse to get his hocks underneath himself and elevate his forehand so that he can more readily jump up and over—rather than "at" the jump. When your horse doesn't respond to the half-halts and continues to run on his forehand—long and low and out of balance—he's not answering your "telephone call," and he's more likely to hit the jump or fall over it.

Unassertive riders are much more likely to get into these kinds of dangerous situations than are riders who "make it happen."

However, by "assertive" I don't mean "aggressive." Assertiveness is the degree or "loudness" of a *reasonable* request. Aggressiveness is getting short-term results through sheer force or intimidation.

The *assertive* rider builds a foundation of training, so that her horse fundamentally understands the request she is making. They speak the same language, because the rider will have taught the language (the aids) to the horse; she can raise her voice (employ the aids more strongly)—even shout when necessary. (The *unassertive* rider, in contrast, will only whisper or murmur.)

Here's an example. Many horses are spooky about ditches. Small ditches are easy to jump and not dangerous in and of themselves, but try telling that to a spooky horse! When your horse wheels and spins and rears in fright the first time you ask him to jump a ditch, it is assertive to spend as much time as is necessary desensitizing him so that he is willing to jump the ditch because he realizes that the ditch is harmless. This process can include letting him stand quietly near the ditch so he can look at the horrifying thing; following an older, wiser horse back and forth over the ditch until the fear goes away; or even getting off and leading your horse over the ditch on a longe line.

The *aggressive* rider, on the other hand, will do the physical equivalent of screaming.

As a member of the US Equestrian Team, Jane has represented the country internationally in Canada, Holland, Belgium, France, and Germany; she was reserve rider for the US team that won bronze at the Barcelona Olympics in 1992. In 2019, Jane was inducted into the USDF Hall of Fame.

Jane Savoie and the Friesian Menno ("Moshi") enjoying a buoyant canter.

Discipline: Dressage

In addition to earning US Dressage Federation bronze, silver, and gold medals and winning three National Freestyle Championships, Jane has coached Olympic riders from both the US and Canadian Olympic teams. Her popular motivational books and videos have helped thousands of amateurs achieve their riding goals. Jane has also pursued her passion for ballroom dancing over the past decade, practicing and competing whenever she can.

Life circumstances:

Our Worcester, Massachusetts, family was lower middle class and not at all into horses: My mother was a housewife and my dad had a dry-cleaning route.

Hooked on horses when:

I was eight when my parents—for reasons unknown—signed my older sister and me up for ten lessons each at a local hack stable, as a summer activity. My sister liked the lessons and rode for a little while before getting interested in swimming and ice-skating. But I loved it! I taught my dog to longe and built jumper courses for him in the backyard. At a barn in nearby Framingham I mucked a dozen or more stalls a day to get one lesson on the weekend.

I think I got good because:

🔹 I had a burning desire to reach my goal of being chosen to represent the United States in international competition. Without a burning desire, you won't be able to keep going given that there will be inevitable setbacks.

🔹 I was willing to pay the price. For me, that meant losing twenty-five pounds and doing five-in-the-morning sessions at the gym to become the fit, athletic rider my horses deserved. I worked with a professional body builder who trained me with weights and put me on a diet. The hardest part was quitting my three-pack-a-day smoking habit, but I did it.

🔹 I keep learning—every single day—from the horses I ride, and from lessons. I think when you stop learning you can't get good, stay good, or get any better.

🔹 I've never really thought of myself as "good"! I've been trained by the best and I've used my skills. I had to break things down for myself (unlike the truly gifted people who ride by "feel") and that has made me a really good teacher.

🔹 I have had a great emotional support system. My husband Rhett's attitude about the long separations and financial strain when I was training in Europe was, "We are a team." Without that support, when things got tough it would have been easier to say, "This is more than I can deal with."

My most important advice:

Make sure you get a solid foundation by working with someone really good, and riding everything you can sit on. Understand up front that it's a process that requires time, effort, and energy. With a solid foundation, you can be good, whether your goal is to be a good amateur or a top professional.

Jane Savoie

Variants of Courage—Facing Down Your Nerves

Anyone who performs under pressure or in front of the public—whether riders, athletes, actors, public speakers—is apt to suffer from *performance anxiety*. Such nervousness is different from fear, although it can surely feel the same. I don't know many event riders, for example, who aren't nervous before they ride out on the cross-country course. If you were to get a truthful answer, most of them would tell you that they would rather be home cleaning the toilet with a toothbrush than sitting on the tack trunk in front of their horse's stall, waiting to tack up and ride out into battle.

Jack Le Goff once described these states of being as "real fear" and "nervous fear." The chief difference between them is that once the athlete or performer gets going, most of the nervousness goes away.

Real fear is what you might feel in a car whose drunk driver is racing on a narrow road along a cliff edge.

Nervous fear is what you feel moments before walking onstage in front of a large audience to give a speech or act in a play.

Real fear is the fear of real injury, or the real possibility of imminent death.

Nervous fear is often the fear of failure or public humiliation. Unless that audience is really hostile, the actor won't get physically harmed. (Try telling him that, though, while he is throwing up in the toilet five minutes before his entrance!)

Early one morning, I was trying to eat breakfast at the Chester Diner, in Chester, New Jersey, just a few hours before my assigned time to head off on the cross-country course at the Essex Three-Day Event in nearby Gladstone. Some people can eat when they're nervous, but most (myself included) only push the food around on the plate.

The restaurant was filled with chatting, laughing people, and my friend Noel Aderer suddenly asked, "Do you know what all of these people are going to do

It is aggressive to beat him until he jumps the ditch because he is more frightened of you than of the ditch. The aggressive rider, like the assertive rider, gets the horse over the ditch, but the aggressive rider's horse may still be scared of ditches, whereas the assertive rider's horse is more likely to willingly jump a different ditch sometime in the future because his fear of ditches in general has been alleviated.

today, Denny? They are going shopping! That's what normal Americans do on Saturday!"

Whereas I was having one of those moments slightly reminiscent of the gladiators marching into the Coliseum, chanting, "*Ave, Caesar, morituri te salutamus.*" ("Hail, Caesar, we who are about to die, salute you.") I didn't really expect to die that day, or even get hurt, but the whole "fight-or-flight" adrenaline mechanism kicks into gear without truly differentiating among degrees of risk, leaving most performers feeling pretty miserable in the hours ticking down to the moment of truth.

(What did I get out of doing something the prospect of which was stressing me out? The euphoria I experienced on successful completion was directly proportional to the fear I experienced beforehand.)

The fact is that both physical fear and nervous fear are very real, and require real courage to face. That's probably why most go shopping, instead of putting themselves at risk. Theodore Roosevelt (as quoted by William Manchester in *The Last Lion*) pretty well summed up the difference between the many who withdraw from danger, difficulty, and pain, and the relative few who go out to meet them:

> *The credit belongs to the man who is actually in the arena, whose face is marred with dirt and sweat and blood, who knows the great enthusiasms, the great devotions, and who spends himself in a worthy cause; who, if he wins, knows the thrill of high achievement, and if he fails, at least fails daring greatly, so that his place shall never be with those cold and timid souls who know neither victory nor defeat.*

Very few riders of horses are "cold and timid souls." The very fact that you get on a big, powerful, ultimately unpredictable animal pretty well establishes that you already have courage, whether or not you even know it.

The assertive rider may still need to sit deep and use a strong leg and seat to remind the horse that business means business, but the firm aids are reinforcing a reasonable request, the response to which has been built into the horse through proper schooling, which alleviated his fear.

The assertive rider's horse usually responds to the aids more calmly than the horse of an aggressive rider because the assertive rider has taught the aids through repetition, stimulus, response, and reward, rather than through brute force.

An unassertive rider's horse, on the other hand, simply doesn't respond! I've heard instructors say, "Don't let him walk all over you," as an unassertive rider tries to lead a pushy or recalcitrant horse. Horses understand dominance. It's how they learn from other horses. If you are less dominant in your relationship with your horse, you will let him "walk all over you"—not just on the ground, but while you're mounted, too.

■ V. *Courage*: Are You the Lion Pre- or Post-Oz?

Here is the definition of courage: "The attitude or response of facing and dealing with anything recognized as dangerous, difficult, or painful, instead of withdrawing from it."

From the earliest literature down to the present day, courage is the trait most lauded in books, songs, and legends, while cowards are scorned. If it were only so simple! It's still hard to fully understand courage, because it has so many embodiments.

In books like the *Iliad* and the *Odyssey*, "the courage of violence"—in armed combat—is glorified above all other forms, as it often is in more modern books and movies, including the ever-popular tales of the American Wild West. However, if we analyze the definition "facing, rather than withdrawing from" situations that are "dangerous, difficult, or painful," courage becomes a much broader concept than Greeks and Trojans crossing spears in front of the walls of Troy, or two gunslingers stalking out to face each other on a dusty Wyoming street in 1870.

There is the quiet courage of the cancer patient who is somehow able to smile and keep going through enormous fear and pain. There is the person who dares to take an unpopular stand in the face of public scorn and opposition. There is also the courage of the single parent who holds his or her family together through times of loneliness and despair; the compassionate courage of hospice workers who deal with the dying; the daily courage of the air traffic-controller who knows that a single mistake can produce disaster.

Every day, all across the world, ordinary men and women who appear to be anything but superheroes are performing heroic actions.

Most people possess more courage than they know. A line from a song by the band "America" says: "Oz never did give nothing to the Tin Man that he didn't, didn't already have…" (Remember that in *The Wonderful Wizard of Oz*, the L. Frank Baum book later adapted into a blockbuster movie classic by Metro-Goldwyn-Mayer, the Tin Man wanted a heart, the Scarecrow wanted a brain, and the Cowardly Lion wanted courage—all as gifts from the Wizard—because they didn't realize they had these qualities all along.)

Having said that, I also know some people are intrinsically braver than others. Watch a group of young people playing for a while in all kinds of situations, and it will be obvious that there are always one or two who are more adventurous, more prone to risk-taking than the others

When it comes to riding horses, I think this discussion of courage brings us right back to the square peg/round hole analogy. All horse sports require courage, but some require an *enormous* amount. Compare a slow trail ride on a sunny morning with sitting on one of thirty milling Thoroughbreds lining up for the start of England's Grand National Steeplechase.

Obviously, these two examples are extreme ends of the spectrum, but even the easiest and quietest horse sports involve risk, which means every rider will need a degree of courage. Bear in mind, too, that courage is what you need for any task at hand that frightens you. Galloping across the open prairie may be an easy morning lark for a fit, agile, seventeen-year-old cowgirl, but that same lark takes on totally different proportions for a sixty-year-old rider coming back from a major illness or injury.

As an aside, does courage imply being scared of something but doing it anyway? Is someone courageous when what she does doesn't scare her? For example, is someone who is terrified of heights, but ventures onto a cliff edge to save an injured hiker, exhibiting more courage than a high-steel worker (who climbs around all day on the girders and beams of skyscrapers, totally unaffected by any fear of falling) who performs the same act? I think most of us would say the answer is "yes"—doing something that doesn't cause you any fear doesn't require courage.

True Grit

A character trait closely related to courage is summed up by the old-fashioned phrase "true grit." Also called "heart," it refers to a mental and spiritual toughness that somehow propels its possessor through all manner of hardships and disappointments. True grit is for people who just don't know when it's time to give up. True grit defies logic and keeps going when logic would declare, "Whoa, stop, enough already!"

Most really great competitors have it, and it's an especially key ingredient in the horse world, because there's almost always something going wrong! The horse's big and powerful appearance conceals the sad reality that much about him is fragile. It's those tiny legs and little hooves supporting that thousand-pound body that so often lets him down. And as the horses we ride go lame, our dreams come crashing down with them. If you don't have what it takes to clamber out of the ashes of your burned-out dreams, time and again, you'd better take up golf.

Mary Alice Brown, a friend of fifty years, was staying in a bed-and-breakfast while in England to watch the Badminton Three-Day Event. When Mary Alice told her landlady the purpose of her visit, the elderly woman replied, "'Osses! I know all about 'osses! Me 'usband 'ad 'osses! 'Osses is always lame. And when they hain't lame, they cough!"

And they do one or the other, usually, about two days before the biggest day of your life. That happened to me just the day before the vet check at the Montréal Olympics in 1976. We had our last gallop on Tuesday morning, and when I took Victor Dakin out of his stall that same afternoon, he was lame on his left foreleg. Mildly lame, from who knows what, and sound three days later—but we didn't get to ride on the team that won the Olympic gold. If you can't bounce back from that kind of disappointment, you don't have what it takes.

The same can be said of coming back from personal injuries. If you ride enough horses, over enough years, it's not a question of whether you are going to get injured, but when, and how badly. I've had seven broken ribs, a separated shoulder, a collapsed lung, two broken hips (one of which required a partial replacement), a fractured eye socket, and God knows how many bumps and bruises. Lots of riders have been hurt much more permanently than I have, and, of course, sometimes you die.

These are the realities of horse sports, and not only in racing and eventing—the fast-paced sports filled with violent action. Some of the worst injuries happen in the most apparently innocuous circumstances, while mounting or dismounting, or while happily gazing into the middle distance on a Sunday trail ride in June: A bird darts up, your horse does a 180-degree spin, and you slam into the gravel road. Yes, you can wear a helmet, and be reasonably smart, but horses are big, quick, and unpredictable.

Can you bounce back from failure, disappointment, injury, and loss? That's the sort of tough resilience that can be called "true grit," and in horse sports, you have to have it.

■ VI. *Work Ethic*: Kick the Couch Potato Habit!

It's the year 1856, and you live on a subsistence farm in central Vermont. You have a pair of Holstein oxen for the really heavy work; a Morgan-cross horse for the lighter work and transportation. You have chickens, a hog, and twelve milk cows. Every day is unrelenting toil, from early dawn until well after dark. You don't have dental care, but no one else does either. There is no anesthesia for broken bones, no plumbing, no electricity, no telephone, no nearby hospital, no fast transportation, no paved roads, no heated vehicles. But because this is all you have ever known, and because all your neighbors live in essentially the same manner, you consider your life normal and natural.

If any of us, living on those same farms (as I do now, one hundred and fifty years later), were suddenly subjected to those same conditions, we would most likely think the experience intolerably hard and harsh.

So the question arises, "Can I have at least a glimmer of the work ethic that those farmers had, in the absence of the necessity that drove them to labor from dawn to dark?"

I am convinced that the apparently advantageous, privileged "life circumstances" that I talked about in chapter 3 are sometimes a *disadvantage*, because they deprive children of the *privilege* of struggle.

Privilege? Yes. In fact, many parents of previous eras really understood the importance of instilling a work ethic—whatever their children's life circumstances. For instance, I love the story about the teenage son of President Calvin Coolidge (himself the product of a New England farming heritage), who had a job in the tobacco fields when his father was

Mary has ridden for Great Britain at six Olympic Games, sharing in a team silver medal in London in 2016 and in Athens in 2004, and a team bronze in Beijing in 2008. Mary's international career also includes a team gold medal won at the World Equestrian Games in 1994 (The Hague), a team silver at the 2006 Games (Aachen), and a team gold in 2010 in Kentucky.

Mary King celebrates after securing the gold medal in eventing for the team from Great Britain at the 2010 World Equestrian Games in Lexington, Kentucky.

Mary and Imperial Cavalier tackle the cross-country course at WEG 2010.

Discipline: Eventing

A two-time Badminton winner (1992 and 2000), Mary has won five British national titles and four British open championships. She has earned four European team gold medals (1991, 1995, 1997, 2007) as well as individual bronze (1995) and silver (2007). Mary won the Kentucky Three-Day Event with her homebred mare King's Temptress in 2011.

Life circumstances:

When I was born in Newark-on-Trent, neither of my parents was the least bit horsey. My father, a naval officer, had suffered a severe head injury in a motorcycle accident before I was born. This changed him as a person; he needed to stay at home, where he could have a familiar daily routine.

Hooked on horses when:

I'm not sure where I got my love for horses. But the vicar in our village had a pony, and that's where my riding career began. That pony used to bite and kick—not very nice!—but then the vicar got another pony that was a bit more pleasant. It was somewhat big for me, but I enjoyed riding him; he was a kinder horse.

I think I got good because:

❧ After I got my own pony when I was twelve, I became a very keen member of the Axe Vale Pony Club. I worked my way up through the Pony Club tests and eventually passed my "A" test—the top level.

❧ My parents were very supportive. Although my mother wasn't interested in horses herself, she liked to help me; she made the picnic and drove the lorry to competitions, as she still does today! My father didn't like to come to the horse trials, but he was very proud when he read my name in newspaper stories about events where I'd done well.

❧ I wasn't a naturally gifted rider—it took me a year to learn to do a rising trot, and for years I found it difficult to be able to place a horse at a fence. But for some reason I always had this inner drive to succeed in the sport. I think that is the key to any success I've had. I was always keen to do this, even after breaking my neck in a fall ten years ago. Fortunately, the surgeon encouraged me to carry on riding if I really wanted to.

❧ I went to work for former European champion Sheila Wilcox after school, a wonderful learning opportunity.

❧ I have had help over the years from wonderful trainers, particularly Ferdi Eilberg in dressage, and Captain Mark Phillips and Lars Sederholm in jumping.

My most important advice:

First, get as much riding experience as possible. Second, follow your dreams, even if they seem impossible. My own dreams seemed farfetched, from a starting point of a non-horsey family with no money, but I have been able to do what I dreamed of doing.

Mary King

Fig. 14 Mike Plumb always wants to beat you: whether you're on a horse, on a soccer field, probably playing checkers. And the problem is, he usually does beat you, partly because he wants to so badly!

in office. To a young co-worker who said, "If my father was president, I would not work in a tobacco field," Calvin Jr. reportedly answered, "If my father were your father, you would."

A work ethic, though, presumes more than manual labor. Tolerating the daily grind, even *enjoying* the daily grind most of the time—that's having a work ethic.

Many obstacles seem overwhelming and intransigent when you first see them, or even when you carefully evaluate them. It's sort of like the old cliché of draining the swamp, so daunting as to defy completion. What a true work ethic also gives an individual is the fortitude to realize that this goal is going to take a very long time to complete, and that's okay.

It's easy to have lofty dreams, but remember the saying, "It's all right to build castles in the sky so long as you build foundations under those castles." Foundation-building is a very different sort of enterprise than castle-building, though it's an intrinsic piece of the process. There's precious little glamour in digging around down in the cellar, compared to building a turret complete with pennants flashing in the wind. Bouncing around trying to acquire an independent seat isn't the "rush" of riding a victory gallop—but the latter depends on whether you did the former. Having a work ethic is some sort of guarantee, or a least reassurance, that you are likely to be able to do both the cellar work and the tower work.

■ VII. Competitiveness: Winners *Love* to Win and They *Hate* to Lose

Unless you are much better than your opponent, it's hard to beat someone who is desperate to win. It isn't always a matter of who has the greater skill or strength or experience. These are all critical components of victory, but it's almost a cliché that the hungry underdog can win if he wants it more. If the hungry person is also an "upper dog," not an "underdog"—someone who not only wants to beat you but is better than you—you are going to get trampled.

Winners not only want to win; they *need* to win. I've been around plenty of them, and I think that the winning mindset is consuming and all pervasive. For instance, Brigadier General F. F. "Fuddy" Wing, who placed fourth in show jumping in the 1948 London Olympics, seemed to be just a kindly older man with no visible sign of killer instinct when I knew him in the early 1960s. But when I played croquet with sweet old General Wing one evening after supper with mutual friends, he was transformed into Genghis Khan. He destroyed us. If his croquet ball hit yours, he would send yours off the lawn, down the hill and into the street. Once the game was over, General Wing reverted to his kind grandfatherly persona, but I was never fooled again!

Then there is eventer J. Michael Plumb. He has ridden in eight Olympic Games, more Olympics than any other athlete in any other sport (fig. 14). In 1974, when I was part of the US Three-Day Squad preparing for the World Championships, we often played a scratch game of soccer on the lawn of our English bed and breakfast in the summer evenings. Mike's team won. Always. No matter who or how many were on the other team.

In sports, the competitive definition of "win" is to prevail in victory over others. Seen through this prism, a winner may not be the most attractive person to be around, or the happiest, or the most spiritually fulfilled, but she is the person who most frequently rides out of the arena with the blue ribbon hanging from her horse's bridle.

In 1995, the first year that the World Champion Hunter Rider (WCHR) finals culminated in a ride-off between the four riders with the highest cumulative scores from the competition, Havens Schatt—who already had the top numerical score—earned the championship with the highest ride-off score. Havens won the $10,000 USHJA International Hunter Derby in 2019.

Havens Schatt on Lavari at the 2008 AHJF Hunter Classic in Wellington, Florida.

Discipline: Hunter/Jumper

After making a name for herself riding sales horses for Don Stewart Stables in Ocala, Florida, as a junior in the 1990s, Havens continued showing top hunters as a professional. She won the Working Hunter Championship on Caroline Moran's Saint Nick at the 2001 National Horse Show in its final year at Madison Square Garden, the same year she stared her own business, Milestone, with partner Frederic Commissaire.

Life circumstances:

My mom had been a serious rider as a junior and there were horses in our backyard in Ocala from the time I was two. We had a really good pony I could sit on in the paddock, in front of the kitchen window where my mom would watch me. Until I was twelve we just went to small local shows for fun. In fact, if I was giving my parents a hard time, their most effective disciplinary tool was, "Do it our way; otherwise you're not going to the next horse show."

I think I got good because:

◝ Having a parent who was so into it made riding feel natural and easy from the start.

◝ Our location, with horse people all around, made it possible to ride with good trainers and still have a normal home life. When I got to that stage when I didn't want my mom to teach me any more, she sent me to top trainer Christina Schlusemeyer and then to Don Stewart (both local). I continued to have a lot of discipline in my life as a kid, even though I was doing something I loved.

◝ At Don's barn I learned to ride horses whether they suited me or not—and show them! Riding with him got me to all the biggest horse shows.

◝ Connections I made as a junior helped me find positions in really good barns with good horses (such as Marley Goodman's Turtle Lane and the Lindner family's All Seasons Farm) as a professional, so I continued to have really good horses to ride, such as the Lindners' Ashford Castle.

My most important advice:

Practice. Keep on it, don't give up—and don't try too hard to be something that you're not. Try to find a part of riding that you're better at, and become expert at that. Only a handful of people can become top show riders, but there are plenty of other roles for really good riders and horsemen who are part of those ribbons. My partner Fred is a good example. He is awesome at "flatting" the horses, training them at home, figuring out what they need for success in the ring. I couldn't do what I do without him.

Havens Schatt

Fig. 15 There are so many times when it's easier not to…not to condition, not to train, not to compete, not to ride at all. "Not" is a word *not* to have in your lexicon.

The opposite of "to win" is "to lose." Great competitors hate to be losers. In fact, hating to lose may contribute more to their winning habits than loving to win. Various cultures attach greater or lesser values to the whole "win/lose" mystique. American culture glorifies winners and derides losers, which stimulates the competitive drive in those who are competitive already.

There are great trainers who are also great competitors, and these men and women are the most consistent winners. They couple a soft empathy for the horse with an iron will to prevail—a difficult melding—and victory becomes inevitable.

Competitiveness can have a very dark side. Some people will do anything to win—even if it means causing immense pain and distress to the horse, or involves illegal drugs and abusive methods. This "dark side" is reflected in the fact that most of the major horse associations have pages of rules concerning illegal drugs, equipment, and abusive training;

various penalties for rule infringement; and an array of procedures for hearing committees, fines, censure procedures, and even lifetime exclusion from the sport for the worst offenders.

All of this is necessary because some riders' competitive drive blinds them to all considerations of fair play and humane decency to their horses. Analyze your competitive drive with a watchful eye. It can be the ultimate "double-edged sword," cutting both *for* you and *against* you.

■ VIII. *Focus*—And *Not* with Your Camera

Winston Churchill defined a fanatic as one "who won't change his mind and won't change the subject." As a definition of focus, that's perhaps a bit harsh, but most of my friends who are great riders don't miss Churchill's description by more than a whisper. Maybe they'll change their mind a little about new schooling methods, but the intensity of their focus borders on fanaticism.

Real riders' focus drives them like a cattle prod. They ride when it's cold, they ride when it's raining, they ride after work, they get up at five in the morning to ride, they ride when they don't feel so well, and they ride when they don't really feel like riding for any of a hundred reasons (fig. 15).

More casual riders may come home from work on a gray and cold winter evening, and sit down in the recliner for a couple of minutes before they go up to change into their riding clothes and head out to the stable and indoor ring. But that chair feels so good, and the weather feels so bad, more casual riders might say "the heck with riding today."

This scenario simply doesn't happen with focused riders. Perhaps they have developed failsafe mechanisms to prevent these kinds of letdowns, mechanisms you can adopt as well. There are choices you can make to outwit these little traps. Don't let lethargy get the upper hand! You can trick yourself into more productive choices.

For instance, never sit down for "a couple of minutes" to look at that newly arrived magazine before heading for the barn. Never ever have "one quick beer." In fact, never even stop at home; drive directly to the barn and change there. Whatever the strategy, your focus on the goal is the driving force.

Success-oriented riders focus on long-term objectives, but set short-term and intermediate goals as rungs in the ladder. Focus and goal orientation are so inextricably interwoven that in my mind they are like that line in the old song "Love and Marriage": "You can't have one without the other."

A goal is what you focus on. Anyone who is going to become a good rider will necessarily have hundreds of goals. To acquire that elusive independent seat is a goal; to acquire "good hands"; to buy a very talented horse; to find a top-notch riding instructor; to ride in the Quarter Horse Congress, Madison Square Garden, Dressage at Devon, the Tevis Cup, Rolex Kentucky. These are goals.

Setting goals is the easy part. Then you chip away at each of them for days, weeks, months, years—and suddenly, there you are. It is focus that keeps you chipping away, and it is the chipping away that achieves the goal.

How do you eat an elephant? "One bite at a time." Without focus, you get sick of chewing those bites.

■ IX. *Detail Orientation*—The Positive Side of Nit-Picking

Meticulous horsemen are more likely to become good riders, because they pay attention to *all* the details, including those of posture and performance. It's not the easiest thing to choose to be meticulous and organized, even "picky" about small details, but if a finished performance really is nothing so much as the sum of a hundred parts, each little part needs to be a polished and finished entity in its own right.

Attention to detail is an acquired attitude, and if you don't already have it you can choose to acquire it. Why does it matter? It matters if you want to become an excellent horseman because excellent horsemen are meticulous and knowledgeable about everything, not just about riding: knowledge of feeding, shoeing, medications, worming, and immunizations all contribute to the final product. So do clean, well-fitted tack and equipment, as well as organized grooming kits and tack boxes, feed rooms, and horse trailers. Not necessarily lavish or expensive, but clean and tidy, just like the detail-conscious rider herself, whose clothes may not be the priciest, but who is always dressed in a neat, workmanlike way.

The Overwhelming Power of Practice

As much as any choice a rider can make, the choice to practice differentiates the few at the top from the many in the huge base of the pyramid, and meticulous riders are willing to put in endless hours of practice

Practice is incompletely understood by the majority of the riders I've taught, even though it's a constant subject of discussion. We all know the saying, "Practice makes perfect," and we also know the saying, "Practice doesn't make perfect; *perfect* practice makes perfect."

We know the words, but not the full meaning beneath the words. When it comes to riding, most people think of practice—we "practice the sitting trot"—in the same way as we practice the piano, and indeed that kind of focused, mechanical repetition is a necessary part of improving. Practicing the sitting trot, riding cavalletti, or spending hours on the longe line without stirrups are the riding equivalent of playing scales on the piano.

On the other hand, when we say that a doctor "practices medicine," and that a lawyer "practices law," we don't mean that the doctor or the lawyer is trying to improve his medical or legal abilities. What we mean is that they "live" medicine and law.

Here is a critical and essential difference between the few riders who get really excellent, and the vast majority who do not: *Average* riders "practice" getting better mechanically, like practicing the piano; *great* riders practice mechanically, but they also *live* their riding. They "practice" riding in the same way that a doctor "practices" medicine; their practice and their life is the same thing.

"But Can I Really Choose My Character?"

I've explained why some character traits are worth cultivating because they have such a strong bearing on how well you are able to relate to horses and improve as a rider. Here are some final thoughts on the common notion that at a certain point in your life, your character is formed and it's who and what you will be, period.

Schools and colleges, which are among the major institutions in most countries, certainly address the idea that knowledge is "improvable."

Similarly, gyms, sports programs, health clubs, spas, even weight-loss programs, all exist to help people develop change and develop their physical skills or qualities.

But, if someone becomes more patient, or assertive, or braver, or more compassionate—whatever—they tend to develop those traits or emotions as byproducts of "life" rather than from conscious effort. Perhaps this is why there's a tendency to assume that at some point a person "is who she is." Perhaps, because we basically lack systemized, institutionalized programs of character development, we're collectively less likely to think of these aspects of an individual as "improvable." But I believe they are.

There are many more elements of character than those I've addressed in this chapter. As I said at the beginning, I've probably spotlighted those I've had to work the hardest on myself! If I've skipped over your particular demons, try to identify, confront, and defeat them yourself, using similar strategies to those I've suggested. It's a choice that's worth making.

The Body You Choose to Ride With

6

Can You Become a Centaur in the Suburbs?

In this chapter, I am going to talk about choices that can make a great difference in your body, but first let's take a look at your starting point: What kind of physical body do you actually "live in" now? This is the same body you use to climb on your horse, so it surely impacts how you ride! Although we just discussed how riding is 90 percent mental and emotional, it is your body that is your direct physical connection to your horse, and that's where most of your communication with him takes place.

So, are you young or old, tall or short, fat or thin, fit or unfit, agile or awkward, weak or strong, well or unwell? You can add many other pairs of opposites, and every gradation in between that you can imagine.

You will instantly realize that you can't choose to change your age, your height, and possibly, some "givens" about your health. But every other aspect of your physical state is subject to modification—*if you choose to make the effort*.

What you have for a body at the outset has at least some impact on which physical skills you'll be able to acquire for a particular riding sport or discipline, so you need to start by taking a clear, objective look at "what you got." In a "Hollywood-ized" America—the land of sylph-like

Fig. 16 Most collections of eventing photographs will have several shots that feature water. Spraying water, as this Sharpton, Florida, picture of Odessa Contessa demonstrates, creates a dramatic and exciting effect, suggestive of violent action. Once horses learn not to be afraid of water, they tend to leap right into the most daunting looking "arms of the sea."

young "hardbodies," discarded by the media every six to eight years to make room for the next crop to emerge—this can be a daunting task. Still, it makes sense to do so for three reasons.

1   It can tell you whether the body you have right now is appropriate for the sport you are doing right now.

2   It can tell you what you need to change, if anything, to do that sport better.

3   In extreme cases, an honest assessment may convince you that you are in the wrong riding sport—that there's a better choice, a better match, for the body you bring to the equation. A sport to which you're innately better suited could offer you the potential benefits of less frustration, more satisfaction, and better odds of excelling.

The most obvious example of the third point above would be the six-foot-three, two-hundred-plus-pound man who wants to be a steeplechase jockey. "Harry, my friend, I hate to tell ya, but it just ain't gonna happen! There are riding sports you can set your heart on, but being a jockey is not one of them!"

How Tough Is Your Sport?

The riding sports can be roughly divided into those that require a high degree of athleticism, those that require a moderate degree, and those requiring less athleticism. "Athleticism" is subject to interpretation, but within the definition I'd include strength, agility, balance, fitness/stamina/endurance, and quickness.

Generally speaking, the more the horse discipline is a high-impact sport, the more necessary it becomes to have developed an athletic body to withstand the impact. Rodeo sports and jumping at speed, which put you at heightened risk for being "body-slammed," are simply more violent than quieter sports like Western pleasure or dressage (fig. 16).

Two horse sports that require a very high degree of athleticism are saddle bronc and bareback bronc riding. Of all the horse sports, they stand out as being reserved for the athletic elite, riders who can cope with being body-slammed while ten feet in the air on an animal that's likely to stomp them if they come off.

In her story *The Mud Below*, Pulitzer Prize-winning author Annie Proulx describes " …a saddle bronc rider straight, square, and tucked on a high-twisted horse, spurs raked all the way up to the cantle, his out-flung arm in front of him…. The horse's back was humped, his nose pointed down, hind legs straight in a powerful jump and five feet of day-light between the descending front hooves and ground."

Next on the impact scale (from my perspective) comes steeplechasing and flat racing, followed by international-level eventing. Polo might well be high on this list, as would calf roping, although much of calf roping's needed athleticism comes into play off, rather than on, the horse.

A rider's physical toughness can be relative, depending on the sport involved. Juliet Graham was one of the toughest young event riders in the world, back in the 1970s. She rode at Badminton when she was still a teenager, and in 1978 she and her gray mare Sumatra were members of the Canadian Three-Day team that won the gold medal at the World Championships at the Kentucky Horse Park in Lexington.

Not long afterward, Juliet decided to pursue steeplechase racing. She had considered herself a strong young athlete, but she told me that racing over fences required a degree of fitness light years beyond what she needed for even the highest levels of eventing. She began running, biking, and weight-training, and her determined efforts paid off: She had many wins at point-to-points and sanctioned races, including winning the Leading Lady Timber Rider title of the Virginia Point-to-Point Circuit in 1988 on Mocito Bien.

Similarly, Ray Whelihan had been riding three-day events in the mid-1980s and assumed he was pretty tough and fit. Then he got a job galloping racehorses at Finger Lakes Race Track (New York). He later told me that after completing one arduous galloping set, trying to hold together a rambunctious young Thoroughbred who was flinging himself all over the track, he got down on his knees and vomited from sheer exhaustion.

It interests me how few horseback riders take their fitness as seriously as even average high school athletes in almost any sport. Go to the gymnasiums or playing fields of any high school, or even junior high school, anywhere in the world, and you will see kids running, lifting weights, doing pushups, swimming laps—in short, doing whatever is necessary to become tough athletes.

What farm or stable have you ever been to where you have ever seen anything like that? At least there is plenty of manual labor associated with the care of horses and the upkeep of a horse farm.

Even at the top levels of sports as apparently "genteel" as golf, there's been a changed perception about athleticism and physical training in recent years. Tiger Woods, for one, is famous for lifting weights.

How is it, do you suppose, that some participants in riding sports consider themselves immune from the physical requirements that are standard in all other sports? And, given that prevailing attitude, *isn't this a place where you could give yourself an edge if you do pursue fitness?*

Do You See Yourself as an Athlete or a "Horseman"?

Once when I was discussing this question with a group of eventing coaches, the suggestion came up that because riding is a "rich sport," the participants are apt to be physically softer than in most sports. The conversation contrasted equestrian sports to boxing, where so many of the athletes are tough black or Hispanic kids from underprivileged backgrounds; they use athletics as a means of "making it."

Rich, white suburban kids frequently don't do chores or have jobs. They keep their horses at a boarding stable where someone else lugs the water buckets and the hay bales, shovels the manure, and sweeps the barn aisle. These kids don't know what manual labor is because they've never done any. Often their parents don't want them to do any, either, thinking that physical labor is somehow demeaning or below their social status, so the parents are implicit in this "soft, spoiled kid" scenario.

Whatever the reason, I sense that if most of us who ride were to fall into the hands of a tough, demanding coach of almost any sport in almost

A member of the gold-medal-winning USA East team at the 2009 North American Endurance Challenge in Lexington, Kentucky, Meg also won first place and the coveted Best Condition award the same year with Syrocco Gabriel at the FEI Vermont 100. In 2016, Meg received the Maggy Price Endurance Excellence Award.

Meg Sleeper riding Syrocco Harmony at the 2010 WEG in Lexington, Kentucky.

Discipline: Endurance

Meg, a veterinary cardiologist, practiced and taught at the University of Pennsylvania School of Veterinary Medicine until taking a position at the University of Florida in 2016. She was selected as a member of the US team for the 2008 World Endurance Championship in Malaysia. In 2007, she placed first individually in the Zone Team Endurance Challenge, a competition in which her horse also won Best Condition and helped earn the team gold. She was the second fastest US rider in the 2006 Aachen World Endurance Championship, on the USA East gold medal team in the 2001 Pan American Endurance Championship, and also a team member at the 2010 World Equestrian Games and the 2012 FEI World Endurance Championship.

Life circumstances:

I was born in Abington, Pennsylvania, and grew up in Moorestown, New Jersey. My parents loved animals but had no real horse experience (my father is a small-animal veterinarian), and money was tight.

Hooked on horses when:

At age eleven I got riding lessons for Christmas. My father bought me a horse the following year, a grade Appaloosa called Tecumseh ("Tummy") that was a saint. I never looked back! We couldn't afford a saddle for six more months; I rode Tummy bareback every day, fell off a lot, and loved every minute. I did my first competitive trail ride, a 30-mile, with him in 1980.

I think I got good because:

❧ Riding for so long without a saddle was very educational. Tummy took excellent care of me, and we went everywhere.

❧ Competitive trail and (later) endurance were sports in which I could excel with horses whose color (Appaloosa, then later a buckskin half-Arabian for which we paid $540) wasn't a good fit in the local hunt seat shows where I started out competing. The buckskin, Chaucer, hooked me on endurance, and I completed my first 100-mile ride on him in 1989.

❧ Most of the string of really wonderful horses I've competed are horses I've bred and brought along myself, which I think creates a special bond. Actually, most of them are related to Chaucer.

❧ Regular dressage lessons with classical instructor Nancy Clark have made a huge difference in how my horses use themselves, and in my riding.

My most important advice:

Never stop trying to get better and to learn. I take lessons every chance I get, in addition to the regular dressage lessons. If you keep your eyes open, you can learn useful information in the most unexpected places. There are enough hours in the day to get good at your sport even if, like me, you have a demanding day job. You have to decide what you really want to do the most, and do that first.

Meg Sleeper, VMD, Dipl. ACVIM

Fig. 17 Back in the 1950s, word began to trickle back to eastern distance riders about a 100-mile race called the Tevis Cup, which clawed its way up and over Squaw Peak in the Sierra Nevada mountains of California. Because it was considered an ultimate challenge, I'd always wanted to ride the Tevis trail, but it would be almost half a century later when I finally got my chance, on this little Arabian gelding, "Rett Butler," in 2004.

any high school or college, we would be in for a swift and unpleasant wakeup call. We all know the US Army recruiting slogan, "Be all that you can be!" A popular stereotype of riders (not rodeo riders so much, but most of the rest of us) is of people who are soft and coddled. Is the stereotype somewhat accurate? The choice is ours to make.

There are riding sports that require less sheer strength and toughness, but still require fine motor skills and swift reflexes. Dressage, show jumping, and reining would be three of these. One sport that isn't "slam bang" but is still really tough is endurance racing.

As I've gotten older, and shifted some of my personal competitive drive from Advanced-level eventing to 100-mile endurance, I've made an interesting discovery: Eventing can grind you to bits quickly, but endurance racing can grind you up slowly. The end result is about the same! The difference isn't about how much you pay in the end, but the manner of payment. Endurance lets you pay on the installment plan.

It's interesting to analyze the duration of play or competition in the various horse sports, to see what part endurance either does or doesn't play in the equation. In rodeo, the bareback bronc or bull ride lasts for just eight seconds—probably the longest eight seconds of your life, but then, win, or lose, it's over.

A show-hunter round lasts about ninety seconds; a show-jumper round, up to two minutes. A dressage test lasts from about four to six minutes. The two-and-a-quarter-mile 2005 Colonial Cup Hurdle Race was won in five minutes, fourteen-and-four-tenths seconds. A typical Advanced cross-country round at the Three-Star level lasts about eleven to twelve minutes. At the 1974 World Championship Three-Day Event in Burghley, England, it took me about an hour and a half to complete nearly eighteen miles.

A typical 50-mile endurance race lasts anywhere from a fast four hours, thirty minutes to a slow eight hours, depending on the ride. A fast 100-mile endurance race lasts about eight hours. When I placed seventy-fifth out of two hundred and fifty riders in the 2004 Tevis Cup 100-Mile Race, I was in the saddle about twenty-one hours (fig. 17).

Every horse sport requires that you have a body equal to the demands that sport puts on your body. It's really that simple, and it's really that hard. Catlike agility, the flexibility of Damascus steel, tensile strength—these are standard equipment for bronc riders and top stee-plechase jockeys. The power of dogged endurance, mile after mile, from the pre-light of midsummer dawn, to the full moon shining over Auburn, California's Tevis Cup finish—this is the need of the endurance star. Some sports, by comparison, are a walk in the park.

Becoming a Centaur

To truly comprehend what is meant by "a riding body," go to the book-store or library and find copies of old Western prints of Plains Indians by Russell and Remington. If ever there were "centaurs," the half-horse, half-human creatures of Greek mythology, these would be them. Think of what it would mean to live without a saddle, on the back of a galloping

Marsha is a USDF Gold Medalist and two-time winner of the Extreme Mustang Makeover. She is the trainer of Cobra the Mustang—a once wild horse turned World Champion who became a Breyer® model horse in 2017, was named the USEF National Horse of the Year in 2018, and was inducted into the Horse Stars Hall of Fame in 2019.

Marsha Hartford Sapp and Cobra the Mustang have broken ground for wild horses with their fantastic success in the dressage and Western dressage rings. The mutual trust and respect established during the training process is evident in all they have accomplished together.

Discipline: Dressage, Western Dressage, Jumping

A nine-time National Champion and five-time World Champion, Marsha has been a highly successful trainer and competitor in multiple disciplines, as well as coaching the Florida State University Equestrian Team to national success since 2004.

Life circumstances:
I grew up on a dairy farm where working with large animals was a way of life.

Hooked on horses when:
Horses were on the family farm, and riding and jumping became a passion early on. I broke my first horse to ride as a teenager and became interested in the training process. I also showed on the weekends…and I wanted to become as good as possible to do the best for my horses!

I think I got good because:
↪ I was willing to take the time to create a series of steps to follow. I knew that success was a series of goals, and once one goal was met, it was then the time to move on to the next one.

↪ I also learned not every horse could do every task every day. Success in training your horse is knowing what things to work on each day and when not to press for things that are difficult on days the horse just can't do them.

↪ I now know that I will always make mistakes in showing…and I need to learn from those mistakes. I can also plan ahead for problems that could happen and maybe prevent them from happening!

My most important advice:
↪ Hard work beats talent when talent is not working. Practice, practice, repeat! There's no better recipe for success than hard work.

↪ Get up every day with a plan and go for it!

Marsha Hartford Sapp

horse, flying over rocky, precipitous terrain, with just a single strand of rope around his jaw, guiding him solely with knee and thigh pressure because in your hands you are holding a bow or a lance.

Then answer this next question. Could you now, or, if you are older, could you *ever* have imagined riding like that? Because if the answer is "no," I would respectfully submit that you do not or did not have the "ultimate riding body." This requires becoming an integral part of the living, breathing horse, almost as if the spinal column of the horse merges with the spinal column of the rider to create one entity.

Anything less than that is less than the ultimate body—so let's start with the ultimate and work backward. What did it take, back on the Great Plains of the 1700s and 1800s, to become "part" of a horse?

When you are very little, you learn things easily, be they language skills or riding skills. Those Plains Indian boys started riding when they were very small, very flexible, and had the mindless courage of youth.

They spent long hours every day riding over vast tracts of wilderness, climbing hills, fording streams, negotiating rocks and roots and declivities and canyons. They had a warrior mentality as a basic tribal ethic; riders lacking courage either got brave or got passed by. They weren't paralyzed by riding lessons. They learned naturally, by simply letting their body accommodate to the movements of the horse, and they didn't have a saddle between them and the animal to use as a crutch, or in any way to impede their total feel of the living entity beneath them.

If you ask whether it's still possible to become that kind of rider in the twenty-first century, the answer is obviously "yes," but only if you recreate those same conditions. In the primitive cultures of central Asia, where nomads still live on horseback, you'll find riders like this. In parts of the American West, you'll find tough little ranch kids galloping around bareback on their ponies—the same kinds of kids as those who preceded them on that same land a century and a half earlier.

But it's very hard to become a centaur in the suburbs! And it's very hard to do if you start riding when you are thirty, or if you aren't tough, agile, and physical, or if you are scared.

Am I being too blunt? I hope I am, because my job here is to tell the truth as I see it. You don't have to become super fit to attain your riding goals, but the slimmer and fitter you are, the better you can become. It's just reality.

You can still be a very good rider if you aren't a centaur, but you won't be as good as a centaur! It's a fact that we "moderns" have to accept, like it or not.

I think I was pretty much on the way toward being that kind of rider when I was ten, eleven, twelve, or thirteen, but then I went astray and got a saddle and started to get serious! It was my undoing, I suppose, but the buffalo were scarce in Greenfield, Massachusetts, by the mid-1950s, and we weren't at war with any tribe except the Russians (and they had nuclear bombs). So my bareback, high-speed, high-risk adventures began to occur less and less often.

But I've always been thankful that I had all those bareback years, galloping over the hills on Paint with only a halter and a lead rope, because I think even now, fifty years later, hip replacement and all, I could still gallop around bareback comfortably and confidently—assuming I had a safe enough horse!

■ The Horse as a "Shock Wave Producer"

If you carefully watch a horse moving at all three gaits without tack— but especially trotting and cantering—you can discern a lot of motion in the shoulders, through the back, and from the hindquarters. At the trot, diagonal pairs of legs are always on the ground while the other two legs are off the ground, the rhythm of the movement is ONE-TWO, ONE-TWO, ONE-TWO. At the canter, because one phase of each canter stride is a forward-and-upward jump, the rhythm is ONE-TWO-THREE, ONE-TWO-THREE, ONE-TWO-THREE.

Watch this motion very carefully, because when you ride that horse, you are going to feel it all as concussion against your body. It's similar to riding a bicycle across rocky ground, or being jolted by a truck with bad shock absorbers as it bounces along a rough dirt road.

So what are you going to do with all that concussion? Are you going to get bounced around by it, or are you going to figure out a means of absorbing and dispersing the concussion so that it doesn't jolt and bounce and lurch you all over the horse's back?

Many riders—probably most, if the truth be told—never do become "one" with their horse. They avoid the issue as much as possible by posting at the trot and rising into a half-seat or two-point seat for the canter.

The stirrup was a relatively late invention in the long relationship of man and horse, and the stirrup is the primary crutch that allows us to avoid developing what is known as "the independent seat."

"Independent of what?" you might ask, and the answer is not really "independent of having to use a saddle," because—let's face it—this is the twenty-first century, and saddles are here to stay. No, the answer is more specifically independent of having to push against the stirrup to lift your body away from the concussive motion in your horse's back created by the trot and canter.

If you take the average rider, and by "average" I mean if you take every rider from every riding style and discipline—English, Western, stock saddle, saddle seat, hunters, jumpers, reiners, ropers, Morgans and Mustangs, Arabians and Appaloosas and Albanian Warmbloods (Albanian Warmbloods?)—and throw them together in a gigantic blender, and take the average of all the riders in that blend, he or she will not have an independent seat!

Take away the stirrups and ask that rider to walk, trot, canter, and gallop over level terrain (never mind *Man from Snowy River* country) and what will we see? You know darn well we'll see banging, bouncing, lurching, whining, crying, complaining, and abject misery—and all this from a rider who's been riding all of his or her life quite happily, so long as the trusty saddle and even more trusty stirrups were in the picture.

The average rider not only doesn't have the ultimate centaur seat of the Plains Indian buffalo hunter, that rider doesn't even have the beginnings of an *independent seat*.

■ The Independent Seat: What It Takes

So let's face the cold, clear dawn of reality, troops! Number one in our litany of choices of physical skills is simply this: *Do you choose to acquire an independent seat?*

Jack Le Goff, the legendary coach I've mentioned several times already, was a tough trainer, and he could get away with it because you either took what he dished out, or you didn't get to ride for the Team.

Jack liked to ask rhetorically, "What three things do you have to have in order to be a good rider?" Then he would provide the answer: "One—a good seat; two—a good seat; three—a good seat."

Jack once explained to us how *he* had acquired a good seat and, by extension, how most of the cavalry-based trainers of his era had acquired theirs. Most of the leading dressage and show-jumping trainers in the 1950s and 1960s were either former cavalry riders themselves, or had been taught by men who were former cavalry riders. That whole cavalry "ethic" was very strong forty or fifty years ago, and it can only benefit us to understand the roots of a system that produced a seemingly endless string of consummate riders, teachers, and overall horsemen.

Prior to World War II (and even into its early months) the armies of most countries had a cavalry "arm." This tradition really didn't make sense in a modern military environment, as World War I had already demonstrated, but it was a centuries-old custom that seemed integral to training young officers. Furthermore, the equestrian competitions at the Olympic Games were a showcase for the young officers of the various countries' armies, so the cavalry tradition continued until the Second World War proved beyond dispute that the horse was obsolescent against tanks, planes, and machine guns.

■ The Rider as "Shock Wave Absorber"

"Anyway," Jack said, "here's how it worked." Young officer candidates applied for admission to the elite cavalry schools of various countries, such as Poland, Hungary, Russia, France, or the United States. Each candidate might be assigned a string of several horses, and for the next year or so, unless he couldn't take it and dropped out of the program, the young officer would be subjected to the hard realities of what was essentially boot camp for riders: hours of struggling without stirrups, and often without reins, until the gradual process of melding horse and rider into one entity was achieved.

Heed this carefully, please! It's a method in total contrast to today's softer environment, where the traditional situation is reversed in that riding instructors are often "trained" by their students. How?

Suppose I am to teach young Susie and Susie's middle-aged mother how to ride. I need the money that I receive for these lessons, and Susie and her mother have lots of other trainer options besides me. If I take away their stirrups and subject them to the rigorous process of learning to cope with and absorb the concussive motions of the horse's back until they acquire the strength, suppleness, agility, and "feel" that enable them to become one with the movement, how much are they willing to take?

Unless Susie and her mom are two tough cookies who absolutely want to get very good, at some point they will begin warning me to back off. They may complain about how much it hurts, or that it isn't "fun." They can express their displeasure in other, more subtle ways that (if I'm smart) I'll pick up on. I'll realize that unless I want them to bolt to a nicer instructor, one who won't make them suffer and who will tell them how good they are and how nicely they're progressing, I'd better lessen my demands and expectations. (If you think this is the flip side of the earlier discussion about choosing a trainer who keeps you in your comfort zone versus one who actually helps you get good, you are right!)

■ No Way Out

The young officer candidate, like the young Plains Indian boy, had no such recourse. Warrior pride and the hard realities of mounted warfare left them no "out." He either became one with the horse or he didn't become a mounted warrior. Cowboys, Cossacks, Huns, Mongols, Sioux, Cheyenne, Stuart's Cavalry, Custer's Seventh, Alexander's legions—all the mounted cultures in the long, long litany of the relationship consisting of man and horse had the same basic reality. They were in it for survival and they damn well better get it right or they would, very literally, die (which, when you think about it, is a pretty strong incentive).

Is it possible in the twenty-first century to ignore Jack Le Goff's "three things you must have" axiom, and still be a successful rider? You bet. But if you haven't chosen to go through the process of developing an independent seat, you won't be as good a rider as those who have. If your sport lets you post at the trot, or lets you "hover" in your stirrups at the canter, you can avoid Le Goff's key precept and still find pleasure and success, and lots of blue ribbons. But you will know, deep inside, that as a rider you are—in a word—"lacking."

The reason I've spent so much time talking about the seat, which is basically "body melding with your horse," is because *only* when you have an independent seat can the rest of your body be still and calm enough for you to acquire fine motor skills in your arms, elbows, wrists, knees, ankles, lower legs, and feet. You need these fine motor skills for many physical demands associated with excellence in the various riding sports; it's hard to have soft, delicate, feeling hands, for example, if the rest of your body is flailing around and being jolted by the concussion caused by your horse's trot and canter.

I personally believe that the hardest horse sport to gain command of is dressage at the upper levels because it requires such a broad mastery of subtle fine motor skills. Dressage riders don't have to be as tough as stee-plechase jockeys, as gritty as endurance riders, or as brave as bronc riders. They don't need to be able to jump, gallop, throw a rope, or hit a polo ball, but the *best* dressage riders have the most highly developed riding skills of riders in any horse sport ever devised.

By "best," however, I mean *best*. As in any sport, dressage is full of "wannabes" who talk the talk without possessing the skills. There's a tendency to think you can dip your toes into a sport and understand what it takes to do it—hence the saying, "He knows just enough to be dangerous."

For any of the major horse sports, there is a pyramid of excellence. That very peak of the pyramid contains, at any given time, maybe fifty to one hundred riders in the whole world. Of those, perhaps ten to fifteen are the real superstars. Of the superstars, three or four are the Michael Jordans of riding—and this is out of the many thousands who participate in the sport!

The great natural riders throughout history had to become one with their horse out of the harsh necessities of their way of life or their warrior creed, but they didn't have to adhere to any particular posture or style while doing so. There are modern riding sports that require rugged action without requiring any stylistic qualities, and then there are those that require plenty of action with the added challenge that the athlete does so in a particularly graceful or aesthetically pleasing way. Dressage is one of the latter.

In 2015, Buck won a silver medal at the Nations Cup, as well as winning the Richland CIC*** and Jersey Fresh CCI*** with Ballynoe Castle RM. He was the alternate rider for the US Eventing Team in the 2012 Olympics.

Buck Davidson and My Boy Bobby, a 17-hand chestnut Irish Sport Horse gelding owned by Carl and Cassandra Segal, on course at Kentucky Three-Day Event in 2009.

Buck and "Bobby" earned the USET Pinnacle Cup as the highest placing US Rider at the 2009 Kentucky Three-Day Event. The pair jumped clean in show jumping to finish third in a very strong international field.

Discipline: Eventing

Buck was only twenty-two when he came in sixth at the Kentucky Three-Day Event riding Pajama Game, a Morgan/Thoroughbred cross. The following year, they competed for the United States at the 1999 Pan American Games. Since then he has been a constant presence at the top of the sport, riding on the team for the 2010 World Equestrian Games and the 2011 Pan American Games. In 2011, Buck was the #1 ranked event rider in the US. Buck won his second Pinnacle Trophy for Highest Placed US Rider at the Kentucky Three-Day Event in 2013, and had a third-place finish at the event the following year. 2014 wins included Bromont CCI* and Jersey Fresh CCI***.

Life circumstances:

I grew up at Chesterlands, the farm in Unionville, Pennsylvania, where my dad—international eventer Bruce Davidson—had his business. We had a great foxhunt right across the street. And because of who my parents were, I had all those horses to ride.

Hooked on horses when:

I can't say there was a time when I started feeling like, "I have to go riding." While I was growing up, I hated it and didn't want to do it. I played a lot of "guy" sports in school—ice hockey, baseball, football, soccer, basketball—basically, any sport I could do that didn't involve horses. But no matter how many teams I played on, I still had to go to the barn. Now I believe this is the best job I could possibly find, and I love doing it, but it is still my "job." That's where I think I differ from my dad; all he ever wanted to do was ride a horse.

I think I got good because:

➷ I've done pretty much everything there is to do with horses in my part of the world: I've raced over fences, foxhunted, showed hunters, evented…I did anything on all kinds of horses.

➷ I didn't grow up riding in the ring. My dad didn't have time to be out there giving me lessons!

➷ I was never allowed to send my horses away for training; I had to train them myself.

➷ I'm pretty competitive. Once I started doing this and got okay at it, I knew I needed to work harder to be more successful, so the whole thing sort of snowballed and here I am. A couple of years ago, still looking for ways to get better, I felt as if I couldn't really ride any more horses but I could use my "off" time—in the evenings—to improve my fitness by working out. That has made a real difference.

My most important advice:

First, getting good means hours and hours in the saddle, so you need to get on as many horses as possible. Second, you need to be able to do *everything*—all the other work that gives you the opportunity to ride. When I was younger I had to mow the grass, muck the stalls, whack the weeds. My dad said, "You'll never be able to tell anyone how to do something if you can't do it better than they do." As well as knowing how to ride my horses, I have to know how to feed them, how to get them fit, how to shoe them. I talk to everyone I can and try to learn a little from them all. Every day I do all the other things, so I can get more horses to ride, so I can do better.

Buck Davidson

The classical dressage rider must be as one with her horse, but she must be as one while maintaining an elegant, soft, and open posture. She must maintain that posture while performing a series of movements that are increasingly difficult and intricate as she progresses up through the levels.

There are hundreds of books about dressage, and this book will defer to them in terms of "how-to" instruction, but take a good look at just one series of movements performed by the Grand Prix dressage rider who is at the top of her sport. For example, first, read one of the how-to books and find the sequence of aids that is used in dressage to produce a flying change. Now watch a video of someone riding the Grand Prix test, and observe the series of sixteen one-tempi changes in which the horse "skips" across the diagonal of the arena, changing canter lead every stride—quietly, evenly, and perfectly (or at least that is the goal).

Now, get on your horse and try it!

What you must remember is when it comes to difficult physical skills like one-tempi changes, a sliding stop, a pirouette, or a jump over a five-foot oxer, something simpler and more basic underlies almost every movement or action you ask of your horse. When we "build a horse like an onion," each layer of the onion overlaps the layer beneath, down to a tiny core that is, in essence, the newborn foal just breaking out of the placenta—before all the stimuli in his new world barrage him from every quarter. No outer layer of the onion is possible if *any* of the layers below is absent.

In many sports, coaches call this process of laying down the inner layers of the onion "learning the basics." Athletes—human or equine—who have learned and practiced the basics so assiduously that those basics become their normal responses even under stress, are able to begin to add layers to their own onion.

Talent vs. "Plugging"

Learning physical skills so that you "own" them depends upon understanding exactly what is required, and then practicing that requirement until it is a natural response. *Physical skills are acquired through the power of practice.* This basic truth eludes far too many hopeful riders, although I'm not sure why.

I believe people get sick of the tedium of practice, or are discouraged if practice fails to produce swift results (which takes us back to patience and the plateau theory of learning I talked about in chapter 5). Jack Le Goff used to say, "Americans want instant dressage the way they want instant coffee." He saw the roots of much of our failure as a mindset different from one that embraces thorough mastery of skills through long, rigorous programs of hard work.

The famous pianist Vladimir Horowitz, for instance, is credited with saying, "If I don't practice for a day, I know it. If I don't practice for two days, my wife knows it. If I don't practice for three days, the world knows it."

Practice is hard work (fig. 18). Practice means doing the same thing over and over, day after day, week after week, month after month, year

Fig. 18 Good jumping form, like good "anything else athletic," is often the result of hours of practice. Here, King Oscar is making light work of this straightforward fence at Rolex, Kentucky, in 1996. Compared to some of my flailing efforts 25 years earlier, I'm managing to look pretty composed, as well!

The "L" Word

This is where your physical skills are impacted by one of your emotional/character traits, which we discussed in chapter 5. You have your work cut out for you if you are going to master new physical skills, which leads me to talk about the critical "L" word—"L" for lazy!

The word "work" describes what you have to do to get better. The word "lazy" describes the opposite of work. All of us are lazy. The best of us are lazy. It's just that the best of us are less lazy than everybody else.

Of your many choices that you make every day, this is probably your hardest ongoing choice. "How lazy do I choose to be today?"

Look at all the species that surround ours in the natural world, and check out the "LQ"—laziness quotient—of our various earth companions. Cats are really lazy. How many hardworking, industrious cats do you know? Horses are pretty lazy. If you watch a pasture full of horses, they graze and doze, graze and doze. You rarely see horses marching around, trying to get fit, or practicing their piaffe or passage. They run and play only until they get tired, and then they graze and doze, graze and doze.

Birds seem pretty active. They die of starvation otherwise. Death by starvation is a strong motivator for action, and it's the main reason most species of creatures trundle about their daily business. If birds had a plentiful, secure food supply, I doubt we'd see so much winging about. We'd see more of what we see with cats, horses, and cows, which is sleeping. So laziness is a normal state, and therefore, one of the most insidious in its ability to sabotage our attempts to get better at anything. The "L" word, killer of dreams, destroyer of ambitions, is our most constant threat to any hope of improvement.

This threat is one of the best reasons I know for you to have a riding instructor. Her job is to kick your lazy butt! Her job is to drag you kicking and screaming out of your swamp of lethargy. Having a lesson is like going to the library at college to study instead of trying to study in your room, where your bed and TV beckon so invitingly. It's like going to work out at the gym, where other people can see if you aren't sweating.

Riding lessons are a way of forcing yourself to "put out." Yes, you take riding lessons to learn new physical skills, but almost as importantly, you take riding lessons to create a structure and a format that kick you into a work mode and a work ethic.

You pay someone else to make you do what you want to do, but probably won't do, left to your own lazy devices! How many riders do you know who work as diligently at home alone as they do in the structure of a lesson under the eye of an instructor?

after year. Look inside yourself. Do you have the dedication and the determination to choose to work that hard, when you don't know for sure how far that hard work will take you?

This is a mantra I've believed in forever. "If you do keep trying, there is no guarantee that you will succeed, but if you don't keep trying, it is absolutely guaranteed that you will *not* succeed." It's an echo, isn't it, of the Calvin Coolidge quote from chapter 4: "Nothing in the world can take the place of persistence."

Thousands of riders have come to Tamarack Hill Farm over the years to train. Some of them were such naturally gifted athletes it would "make the angels weep," as the old expression goes. It intrigues me, however, how few of the super-talented ones have stayed in the game and become great riders. Of the now-famous names who were once at my farm long enough for me to really get a sense of who they were, it's the "pluggers" who've more often made it than the super-gifted. Talent is great stuff— the greatest, really—but only when it's accompanied by the fierce willingness to plug along, day after day, on cold and dreary days, as well as in sunny weather.

Lots of sports are youth sports. On the other hand, one of the appealing things about the riding sports that require sophisticated skills is that you don't have to be younger than twenty-five to master them. I've just read about four professional football players whose careers are winding down, and they are all in their very early thirties. The thirty-something decade is the best part of most event riders' careers, and eventing is a reasonably high impact riding sport, compared to most of the others. Yes, it takes a long time to get to be a really good rider, but you have a lot of time ahead to use those skills.

You have a lot of time to understand what the Greek philosopher and teacher Aristotle wrote more than two thousand years ago: "For things we have to learn before we can do them, we learn by doing them."

The first time I read that, I said, "Huh?" It sounds like an internal contradiction, but it's really as basic as how a baby learns to walk and talk. An infant doesn't leap to his feet and start to strut around declaiming, "Four score and seven years ago our fathers brought forth on this continent a new nation, conceived in liberty … " You've watched the process, and you've gone through the process, although you can't remember it. Walking and talking begins with falling and babbling, right?

What Aristotle is also saying is that it's not only all right to fail, it's normal to fail. Failure is actually inevitable in the early stages of acquiring any new skill, so it's nothing to fear or be ashamed of. Nor, for that matter, is failure a reason to be screamed at by some instructor because we can't do exactly as she demands!

What actually happens in your brain when you start to learn something unfamiliar by repetition is that tiny electrical currents flash back and forth between little "poles," and the more you do it, the more those electrical circuits make a deeper "groove." (Or something like that!)

If I say to you, "One plus one equals…?" You will say, "Two," without thinking about it. If I ask you to recite the alphabet, you will say, "A, B, C, D, E, F, G…" without a moment's thought. These *conditioned responses* are so thoroughly implanted in your brain that they are automatic. You "own them."

If you pick out your horse's feet very often (and I hope you do), here's what you are likely to observe. You pick up and clean out his left front hoof. Now you go back to his left hind hoof. As you reach down, before you even touch his leg, he picks it up—just another example of "conditioned response," also called "automatic reflex."

I was once standing at ringside when two-time eventing World Champion Bruce Davidson was riding. A spectator commented, "What a beautiful natural rider!" I thought to myself, "Lady, if you only knew how much training has gone into making that look so 'natural.'" Yes, Bruce is a great natural athlete, but he is a *highly trained rider*. He has done the "correct" things so many times that they have become "the way he does business." The "correct" responses are now his "natural" responses, even under intense pressure, because he has learned them so well. The first year he rode, he wouldn't have been able to do those things so "naturally."

The "One Horse" Dilemma

One depressing fact to acknowledge, if you are trying to climb the competitive ladder, is that the riders on the rungs above you are probably practicing more than you are. When I was on the USET, the two top American eventers were Bruce Davidson and Mike Plumb, the individual gold and silver medalists at the 1974 World Championships. They didn't get to be the top riders in the world by not riding. In fact, they probably rode more horses for more hours, and jumped more jumps every week, than their fellow competitors did in a month. How do you catch up with riders like that?

Riders like Mike and Bruce are very prominently in the public eye. If a horse owner is looking for someone to ride and train his horse, and he wants his horse to win, he's apt to call on the services of a known winner like one of them. So now they have even more horses to ride, which means they get to hone their skills even more thoroughly, they win more, they feel confident, they ride better, they get even more horses—and so the snowball rolls.

By contrast, unless the obscure struggler is personally rich, she probably doesn't have lots of horses to jump every week, so she doesn't get dramatically better, so she doesn't win more, and so the "reverse snowball" works against her.

Here's one of the great dilemmas in horse sports: A single horse can handle only so much practice time per day, per week, per month, per year. If you grind on any horse too much, he gets worse, not better. A golf ball doesn't care how often you hit it. A basketball doesn't care how often you shoot it. Athletes in most sports can practice for as many hours a day as their body and psyche can handle, but riders can't unless they have several horses to ride. (Whoops! I told you to win your state lottery, didn't I?)

Years ago a Boston sports writer flew down to Florida on a cold, dreary March day to cover spring training for the Boston Red Sox baseball team. He arrived in the late afternoon after practice was finished for the day, so he decided to take a cab over to the ballpark just to have a look around.

He knew everyone, and he chatted with the trainers and employees who were picking up all the towels and dirty uniforms that were scattered around the locker room. Then he walked through the clubhouse and wandered out onto the playing field. He climbed up the first few rows of the bleachers and stood basking in the Florida warmth, when suddenly he heard the distinctive crack of a bat hitting a baseball.

Fig. 19 One of the first things they'll tell you about approaching a big ditch in front of a vertical wall is, "Don't look down!" That's because the fence appears to be much taller than it really is, since your eye tends to measure the height from the bottom of the ditch, not from ground level where you and your horse actually are. "Stay back, keep your leg on, and look up." Your training must overcome your instinct to look down.

Ambushed by "Wrong Basics"

One way of looking at training, whether of horse or rider, is to think of it as acquiring an ever-growing arsenal of habits. "Habits start out as cobwebs and turn into cables," the saying goes. This is as true of bad habits as good habits, so there is danger in wrong practice. Once you have done something wrong thousands of times, it becomes your normal, natural, conditioned response.

Let's say that when you ride, you look down a fair bit of the time instead of keeping your head and chin up, with your gaze covering lots of territory in front of you and (through peripheral vision) all around you. This is a pretty safe supposition, since just about every rider I've ever seen looks down. Of all the commands shouted by riding instructors all over the world, every single day, none is more frequently heard than, "Look up!"

For most riders, the habit of looking down has become as strong as a steel cable. There are lots of posture and balance problems associated with looking down. Looking down with the eyes is like the first domino in a sequence of negative events. One: The eyes look down. Two: The head follows the eyes, and tilts forward. Three: The shoulders follow the head, and incline forward. Four: The whole upper trunk inclines forward. Very often, as a fifth and sixth domino, the rider's hands come back toward her stomach, and her lower leg inclines forward. That tall, open, balanced, elegant posture is long gone—and it started its vanishing act the second the rider glanced down with her eyes.

Now comes the hard part. Let's assume that our looking-down rider, (which might well be me!) wants to get rid of the bad habit, and replace it with the new good habit of looking up, which leads to better posture and better balance. First we somehow have to erode away that steel cable. In its place we have to introduce a slender cobweb. Then we have to turn that vulnerable little cobweb into a steel cable.

This is a situation instructors face all the time, in which training has to overcome instinct. An instinct, or conditioned response, or automatic reflex—it doesn't matter what you call it—is solidly in place. You "own" it. It's your natural, normal way of doing business, and it's *wrong*. It hinders you from performing well, but that bad habit feels so right! The reason it feels so right is because you've done it ten thousand times. You are going to have to do the new way *twenty thousand* times to even begin to eradicate the bad old way. You're in trouble. It isn't trouble you can't get out of, but you're in trouble just the same. You learned a wrong basic.

What if your riding is a whole bundle of wrong basics? You look down. You hunch your shoulders. Your legs swing all around. Your hands are chaotic and rough. You bounce around at the trot and canter. None of this means that you can't become a better rider, a good rider, or even a great rider, but your work is cut out for you.

A couple of years ago I was discussing this concept that training has to overcome instinct with Sid Shachnow and John Burgess, two friends from Southern Pines, who are also both horsemen.

Sid Shachnow is a retired major general, and was formerly the commanding general of all US Special Forces, so he knows a thing or two about training. Sid told us that when soldiers are suddenly ambushed, the instant and instinctive reaction they have is to turn and run away from the ambush, which actually lessens their chance of survival.

He said that what the soldiers have to be trained to do is to run directly into the ambush, firing their weapons at their attackers.

I got the picture! If soldiers can be taught to run toward incoming rifle fire, riders can be taught to keep their eyes and head up. Training must overcome instinct (fig. 19).

He squinted against the lowering sun, and realized that three men remained on the otherwise-deserted field: a pitcher, a catcher, and one lone player still taking batting practice. Then he recognized the practicing hitter: It was Ted Williams, the greatest hitter baseball has ever known. Long after the youngsters, and the wannabes, and the has-beens had left the field, the one person who theoretically needed it the least was still trying to get better.

If you truly knew the daily life of the best riders in the world, I'll bet you the house that they are like Ted Williams about practice. How are you going to beat them if you don't outwork them?

That's a choice you have to make after an honest examination of your goals and priorities. What compromises are you willing or able to make to get more saddle time? It takes us back to my discussion in chapter 3 about the tradeoffs involved in working in a horse-related job versus an often better paid career outside the horse world.

Swim (or Flounder) in the Vast Sea of Horse Knowledge

7

Two Types of Knowledge: General and Specific

You're reading this book because you want to become a good rider. So stop and consider—in addition to riding itself, how much do you know about training, breeding, shoeing, basic care, veterinary issues, tack, trucking and hauling, nutrition, grooming and show turnout, therapeutic technologies, equine behavior, general management (including stabling and blanketing), the cultural and historic aspect of horses, alternative medicine and...? This list is incomplete but it does give you an idea of how wide and deep the sea of horse knowledge is. And the more you know, the better horseman and rider you're going to be.

In this chapter I've singled out some instances where I see aspiring riders repeatedly bypassing the opportunity to learn. These are only some of the areas of horse knowledge that will help anyone who wants to get better.

◼ General Knowledge

Whatever your horse sport, you have to know how to put on a halter. Then you have to know how to lead your horse. You have to know how to put on his saddle pad, his saddle and bridle, and know how the various straps and buckles work, and how tight or loose they should be. You have to know how to mount and dismount, how to get your horse to go forward, to stop, and to turn right and left. Unless you only plan to ride your horse at home, you also need to know how to load him into a trailer. Once he's in, you have to know whether to put up the butt bar before you tie him, or tie him before you put up the butt bar, and why.

You need to know how to get your horse to calmly pick up all four feet, and how to tell if his shoes are secure or loose. You need to know, by watching your horse trot, whether he is sound or lame, and if he is lame, you need to know which leg is sore.

You need to know what is and is not appropriate to feed your horse, and how much to feed him, and when to feed him.

I could go on and on, but you get the picture. This is general horse knowledge that every good horse person possesses. Someone who has never been around horses won't know any of this, but there are thousands of little kids still in grade school who know all of it, and much more. Why do they know it? Because they have learned it, sometimes from books and videos, but usually because someone has taught them, either in 4-H or Pony Club, at some lesson or boarding stable, at home or from a friend. All this basic, general horse knowledge is known by endurance riders, dressage riders, and by the yak herders in Tibet who ride little Mongolian ponies (except the yak herders ride from one campground to another; they don't use a horse trailer).

◼ Specific Knowledge

Then there is knowledge specific to a discipline, sport, or breed. Let's take a very simple example, using two of the sports that I do, endurance riding and eventing. You need the kind of global knowledge I've just cited to be good in both endurance and eventing, but then you get to the specialized areas. An endurance rider does not need to know how many feet there are in a two-stride in-and-out. An event rider does not need to know how to give his horse electrolytes at a water stop. An endurance rider does not need to know how to ride a shoulder-in. An event rider does not need to know what is meant by the statement, "Your criterion at each hold will be sixty-four."

Neither the event rider nor the endurance rider will need to know how to drive through cones, how to ride a reining pattern, or how to persuade a horse to slow gait and rack.

You can't worry about the areas of special horse knowledge that don't apply to your sport; the wide, deep ocean of knowledge I described in the first paragraph is waiting for you whatever your discipline. You have to say, "This is what I've decided to get good at, and I'm going to be all I can be in my sport. If someday I choose to pursue a different sport, I'll have a whole new body of knowledge to acquire, but for now I'd better dig deep into what's available." Digging deep means seizing every opportunity to learn.

Dependents vs. Independents

I've been teaching the sport of eventing for nearly forty years. During that time, I've asked literally *thousands* of young riders (and plenty of not-so-young ones, too), "What are your goals?" Many of them have replied, "To win an Olympic gold medal." That's a nice, straightforward answer, don't you think? And since the odds of winning one are about one in a million, you would think, would you not, that those young "eager beavers" would assiduously study the task at hand?

Call me a cynic, a pessimist, a grouch, a curmudgeon, or whatever you want, but I can tell you that about one in three hundred of them have the vaguest clue about the sport that they desire to conquer.

Take the simple fact that stadium-jumping course designers don't scatter jumps at random, but have very specific goals in mind, based upon the fact that the average horse's canter stride is about twelve feet long. Course designers know that a cantering horse will take off approximately six feet in front of a three-foot, six-inch jump, and he will land approximately six feet beyond the jump. Thus, course designers usually work from the premise that the "normal" distance in a one-stride in-and-out is twenty-four feet (six feet for landing, twelve feet for the stride, six feet for the takeoff). For a two-stride combination it's thirty-six feet; for a three-stride combination it's forty-eight feet, and so on. Everybody who aspires to know anything about jumping needs to know these mathematical facts.

Liz was named traveling reserve rider for the US Eventing Team for the 2019 Pan American Games in Lima, Peru, and reserve rider for the Team for the 2018 World Equestrian Games in Tryon, North Carolina. She was part of the 2019 Nations Cup Team in Aachen, Germany.

Liz Halliday-Sharp on Deniro Z at Luhmuhlen CCI5* in 2018. "This horse is just incredible," says Liz. "I feel so lucky to be his jockey."

Discipline: Eventing

Liz has competed on multiple Nations Cup teams for the United States, finishing with a team silver in 2015. She has won twenty-one international events in her career and is ranked in the top thirty in the world. In 2018, Liz finished eighth in the Luhmuhlen CCI5* with Deniro Z. A keen competitor, she has also pursued a career as a professional racing driver in the sports car and GT endurance disciplines.

Life circumstances:

I grew up in California, and for years I rode any horse I could get my hands on, from old Quarter Horses to off-track Thoroughbreds. My parents really made me work for it if I wanted to ride, which I am forever grateful for! My first horse was a cheap OTTB chestnut mare—she was totally wild and certainly taught me a lot. We made our way through Pony Club together, and I really learned that eventing was the equestrian sport that I loved the most. At the same time my dad was very much involved in car racing. His dream was to have his kid in a racecar, too, and I was lucky enough to get my first shot at motorsport when I was sixteen. Dad and I raced together in the United States for a few years, but when I got the opportunity to go and work for William Fox-Pitt in England in early 2000, a whole new world of eventing and motorsport opened up for me. What was meant to be one year away become nearly twenty years in the United Kingdom, many of which were filled with both eventing and racing at the top professional level simultaneously. I made the tough decision a few years ago to step away from car racing and to firmly dedicate myself to my eventing pursuits, which has ultimately paid off with better results and more focus on my goals.

Hooked on horses when:

For as long as I can remember, I wanted to ride horses. I come from a non-horsey family, but there was a small stable down the road, and after a lot of begging, I was allowed to have my first riding lesson at the age of eight, and I was totally hooked!

I think I got good because:

➷ I try to always keep learning and improving. I think that even when I am winning there are always ways that I can be better. I try very hard to learn from both the good results and the bad, and to be open to coaching and lessons from lots of different people. I really think you can always learn something from another talented rider or trainer.

➷ I aim to always work hard and I am stubborn! I think that certainly in eventing the highs are high and the lows are even lower…. It's important to be tough in your mind and to be a fighter. I try to do as much work as I can myself with all my horses so that I really build a partnership with them and keep my fitness up. I think that all the ups and downs in the sport have served to make me stronger. Each time you find a way to pick yourself up and fight harder and be positive after a tough result only makes the good days and the successes feel better!

➷ Treat every horse as an individual and be patient and unemotional in the training process. This is something that I continue to work on all the time. I try to let the horses "tell me" what they are ready for. Moving horses up a level when they show that they are ready is just as important as knowing when to give them a break. Good horses enjoy being challenged, and at the same time, I think that it is so important to let horses tell us when they are ready for a mini holiday—sometimes a young horse will reach his greatest potential when he has stepped up a level, tried his hardest, and then is given a few weeks off to digest what he has learned.

My most important advice:

Treat every horse as an individual and learn to train each in the way he needs…and never, ever give up fighting for your goals…and be stubborn about it!

In addition to knowing the basic math about distances, it's also important to have the "tools" to figure out what the actual distance is between any two fences—at a show or in a training arena. The obvious and best answer would be to measure these distances with a tape measure or a measuring wheel, but no one uses those devices at competitions. This means we have to be able to pace the distances, by standing with our backs against one jump and counting how many of our three-foot strides we take to arrive at the following jump. If we take eight three-foot strides, we know the jumps are three times eight—or twenty-four feet— apart, a perfect one-stride distance for the average horse.

However, just as many jumper riders fail to know the basic math, so many of them lack an accurate three-foot stride. This is easily reme- died by practice. Put a piece of duct tape on the floor of your barn aisle every twelve feet, or put pegs in the ground twelve feet apart (measured precisely with a tape measure) and walk it and walk it until *your* stride is three feet. But you have to actually practice this, and most riders just don't do it.

Which brings to point another good way to get that "edge" in a jump- ing sport: Do and learn what others are too lazy or disinterested to achieve!

Just as most high school graduates don't go to Harvard, so most rid- ers don't learn a fraction of what they need to learn if they are to become expert in some area of riding. And I wonder if we teachers are partly to blame for not doing more to inspire them. I have to admit I don't stockpile "textbooks" to hand out, books like Jim Wofford's *Gymnas- tics: Systematic Training of Jumping Horses*, Frank Chapot's *Winning*, Bill Steinkraus' *Reflections on Riding and Jumping,* or any book by George Mor- ris—the books that I keep referring to myself. Perhaps I need to create a kind of lending library for my students, and augment my lessons with written or oral quizzes and tests.

Each horse sport's vast body of knowledge is (these days) often on well-presented DVDs, as well as books. Remember our earlier discussion on page 47 about different learning styles? Some "left brain," or audi- tory, learners do very well by reading. Others do better watching DVDs. Others ingest the information better if it is filtered through an instructor, mentor, or friend, and imparted verbally. But it really becomes the *choice of the individual learner* to pick the learning style that works, and then go and learn it!

As I tell my riders, "Go to any competition, and watch the groups from the various stables walking the lines between the jumps." There, instructors are followed by a swarm of students (their "ducklings"). "There are three slightly short strides between fences 5 and 6," intones each instructor. "Three short strides," parrot the ducklings. I ask my students, "Do you want to remain dependent all your life, only competent to do this when there's someone to tell you how, or do you want to be able to think for yourself?"

From Clueless to Clued-In

I've been reading *Some Horses* by Thomas McGuane. It's basically a book of essays, many of them about cutting horses. I know next to nothing about cutting, except what I've seen briefly on television. I don't know how to ride a cutting horse, or how to train one. I don't know the rules for cutting-horse contests. I don't know what equipment cutting horses wear, or what the riders wear, or what kind of saddles they use. When it comes to the sport of cutting, except that I know how to ride a horse, I'm a complete novice.

Suppose I wanted to explore this new world more fully. What would I do? One way would be to go online to locate a cutting-horse trainer who takes students that don't own their own cutting horses, go to the trainer's facility, and start riding. But that's a pretty extreme initial option. Instead, a more reasonable introduction is to go online and find some books, magazine articles, and videos to read and watch.

Then, armed with "just enough knowledge to be dangerous," I'd probably go to a cutting-horse show and start asking questions. This might lead me to a training stable, or some such hands-on opportunity. Then, depending upon my degree of interest, I might become more deeply involved in my new sport.

In some ways this process would be easier for someone like me, because I already know a lot about horses—how they function, what they

Devin and Eddie Blue won team gold at the 2018 World Equestrian Games in Tryon, North Carolina, and a silver medal at the 2018 World Cup Final in Paris. The pair were members of the bronze-medal-winning team in the FEI Jumping Nations Cup CSIO5* at CSIO Sopot (Poland) that year, and as part of the U.S. team at CHIO Aachen (Germany), they jumped double clear in the Mercedes-Benz Nations Cup.

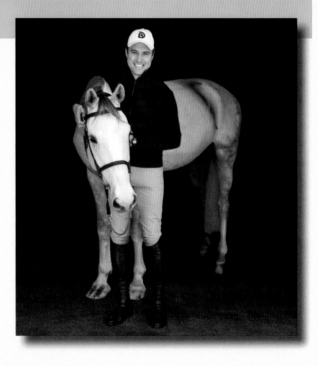

Devin Ryan with Eddie Blue, who he found as a four-year-old and rode to a team gold medal at the 2018 World Equestrian Games in Tryon, North Carolina.

Discipline:
Show Jumping

Devin's successes with Eddie Blue, the horse he found as a green four-year-old, include a second place finish in the 2017 $35,000 Savaro 1.50m at Live Oak International CSI3*, and winning the $30,000 6-Year-Old Young Jumpers Championship at the Hampton Classic in 2015, as well as the 5-Year-Old Young Jumpers Championship there in 2014.

Life circumstances:

Born and raised in New Jersey, some of my earliest experiences with horses took place at a farm in Sussex County that my grandfather owned. I started riding under the tutelage of Dolores Hunt. A year later, I began competing in the United States Pony Club Tetrathlon events. Through my experiences eventing in Pony Club, I took a great liking to show jumping and took a position as a working student for George Morris, Chris Kappler, and Jeff Cook at Hunterdon.

Hooked on horses when:
I was thirteen years old when I discovered my love for horses.

I think I got good because:
↳ During my time working at Hunterdon, I gained a strong understanding of the show jumping industry, and most importantly, how having a program is essential for success. In order to bring out the best in both riders and in horses, at any level of the sport, it is vital to have a consistent program. George, Chris, and Jeff made it very clear to me that attention to detail is also essential for creating the ideal program.

↳ From 2002 to 2003 I worked for a horse dealer and breeder named Alan Waldman in Holland. At "Stal Waldman" my eyes were opened to both a European style of horse showing, as well as how farms start and develop young horses. In the States, my riding opportunities consisted of exercising "made" show horses, and I had never ridden a young unbroken horse. I quickly learned at Stal Waldman that "getting the job done" was my most important skill. Getting the job done was based on feeling, not forcing the horse to complete the task. You get much more out of a horse physically and mentally with feeling, which in turn gains a horse's confidence and trust. Alan imbedded that philosophy in me while developing young horses.

↳ For most of my career I have not had the means to purchase horses that are ready to step into big classes. In order to jump at a higher level, I have had to develop young horses from the beginning of their careers up to their highest potentials. Having experiences with green horses helped me develop my "feel" much faster than if I had ridden made horses. The first bigger classes that I competed in were on horses that had never competed at that level either—the feeling and trust that I cultivated during younger years of development played an enormous role in my success and ability to navigate a more difficult level of the sport for the first time.

My most important advice:
Your horse is your best teacher. Sometimes the most difficult horses have the most to give back to you, and giving up should never be an option. Read your horse's signs and signals, and by doing so, you can earn his trust and build a relationship that will bring you closer to your goals. You won't always have your dream horse, but it is important to ride as much as you can, no matter the quality or ability of your mount. Every horse teaches you something, and passing up an opportunity to ride and listen to your horse might be passing up learning something that could help you move forward in your career.

Devin Ryan

eat, how they lead and load, how to put on boots and saddle pads and saddles and bridles—general knowledge not specific to cutting. If I don't shoot my mouth off and come on like some expert, it would probably be recognized that I am not a total horse neophyte.

I also know a fair bit about the trainer-client relationship, how the general system works. But even if I didn't know how to work the system, I think I could get into cutting some way, somehow, just by making contacts. One contact usually leads to another, and every person can answer some of your questions. Answered questions bring you knowledge, and knowledge is what you need to get started in any new enterprise. Knowledge is always what you'll need, but at the outset, you really do need to have a clue!

When you've been in any business for long enough to be legitimate, it becomes pretty easy to spot clueless people. If someone is genuinely interested in learning, and sets out to gather information in an energetic and systematic way, that person doesn't have to stay clueless for very long. It may take years to become a master, but most of us can get through the entry-level acquisition of knowledge pretty readily.

What's embarrassing (or annoying, depending upon your degree of tolerance) are clueless people who come on like experts but reveal, every time they open their mouths, their absence of knowledge. If you want to be accepted and helped in this brave new world you are entering, a little humility goes a long, long way in persuading people to clue you in!

If I buy a belt with a big buckle, get a black Western hat, put on my best drawl, mosey on up to some cutting-horse experts, and say something profoundly stupid like, "Boy, don't that little dun have a lot of cow in her?" they are just going to roll their eyes and think, "Who is this idiot?"

I'd be better off with my group of cutting horse competitors if I said something like, "Boy, in all the years I've been around horses, I've never seen any with the incredible natural instincts that cutting horses seem to have. Is that bred in, or trained in? I'd sure like to know more about this sport." Just like the minister approached by the repentant sinner, those cutters would see in me a possible convert to the fold, and would be much more likely to embrace me.

Become a Student of Your Sport

The knowledge you need is out there, and while we should read books and watch good videos, they don't usually impact us as well as words from an expert's mouth—good old human interaction. The problem is, though, that no matter which path you may choose to gain more knowledge about your chosen sport, each path requires that you become a student.

"Student" is derived from the word "study," which *Webster's* defines as "1. the act or process of applying the mind in order to acquire knowledge, as by reading, investigating, etc. 2. careful attention to, and critical examination of, any subject, event, etc."

How many riders do you know who study the vast field of riding with anything approaching "the careful attention, the critical examination" that is routinely expected of the student in law, medical, or engineering school? Doesn't it strike you that a great many riders are intellectual "dabblers," rather than ardent students?

Let me give an example from my own experience, one I've watched over the years countless times. A riding clinic usually entails bringing a guest instructor to a local stable, riding club, or organization. The instructor is typically a well-known professional in his or her field, recognized enough to draw paying customers to the clinic. Often the clinic is in a place that is remote from the epicenter of the clinician's sport.

For the moment, let's assume the clinician's sport is show jumping. So here we are in East Nowhere, USA, and standing in the local indoor arena is a former Olympic rider who once wore the red coat with the blue collar of the United States Equestrian Team.

The chance of earning the right to wear that coat is one in many thousands—and a rider with the enormous skills to have gotten that chance is right here.

East Nowhere is not a hotbed of Grand Prix show jumping like a Wellington, Florida, or a Warendorf, Germany, so wouldn't you suppose that anyone in a hundred-mile radius who professes the desire to become a good show-jumping rider would be sitting in the first row, as primed and ready as an ambitious student sitting in the classrooms of the world's medical or veterinary colleges?

If you think that, you would be wrong. For a hundred and one reasons, many local riders, including local instructors, won't be there. In fact, more frequently than I suspect we realize, the local riders won't be there *because* they will have been "warned off" by the local instructor. This isn't as strange as it sounds. I think that being a local riding teacher can be a tough, competitive, hardscrabble business, and any time her credibility is called into question, especially by an "authority figure" in a public forum, she is in danger of losing students.

Different clinicians sometimes use very different methods to achieve the same results. Suppose I (as the "local instructor") have been working with my student to develop an eye for a distance to a fence, and now the clinician tells him, "Don't interfere! That's the horse's job, not yours!" It would be easy for my student to begin to doubt my validity, especially if the clinician has recently returned from a highly publicized and successful USEF foray into the heart of European show-jumping competitions.

Ideally, though, local instructors go to such clinics, at least to watch, and take their students with them. They can explain to their students beforehand that there are many ways to teach the same skills, to allay any doubts and fears the clinic might provoke. They can also explain one further truth—that sometimes we can hear the same thing over and over and over, and just not get it. Someone else—maybe a clinician—says the same thing in a slightly different way, and, presto! Suddenly the elusive concept becomes clear.

So let's just say that local riders, and a few local instructors, do decide to either audit or ride in this clinic. Watch closely. Do they treat the clinic like a normal lesson, or do they treat it like a series of college lectures? If I am riding with the clinician at one o'clock on Saturday afternoon, and nine o'clock on Sunday morning, do I show up at noon on Saturday and at eight on Sunday, just in time to tack up my horse for my "lesson," and then depart shortly following the lesson's conclusion?

Or am I there from early each morning until late each afternoon, armed with a notebook and determined not to miss a word of this learning opportunity? Remember, this clinician is the "real deal," a rider who has defied the enormous odds against ever making it to the top echelons of the riding world, and who has an enormous amount of information that I do not possess.

Now I grant you that just because someone has been a great rider doesn't guarantee that the rider is a gifted teacher. One of the worst clinics I ever watched took place at Charles Bronson's farm in Hartland, Vermont, years ago. The clinician was one of the world's most gifted riders, a USEF show-jumping superstar. But he wore street clothes (he wasn't about to climb on anybody's horse to demonstrate anything) and leaned against the door, a cigarette dangling from his mouth, directing in a bored monotone, "Jump that, jump that red one, jump the oxer. Good. Next."

But suppose the instructor is as talented a teacher as he or she is a rider—the information-imparting equivalent of a gifted college lecturer, one who has distilled and synthesized years of experience into clear, concise information and wants to convey this wisdom to the clinic partic-ipants and auditors. Are you there as a keen "college student," or are you there to see and be seen, to chat with your buddies as your attention drifts in and out on the clinician's words, techniques, corrections, and solutions?

I can guarantee that if you go to a two-day clinic from dawn to dusk, notebook in hand and brain in gear, you will come away with more mate-rial than you will even be able to assimilate. You will have been "trying to drink from a fire hose." And your friend—the one who wandered in and out of the exact same clinic—will have squandered an enormous learning opportunity.

Learning is interactive and it requires something very difficult, namely critical thinking. Remember what Henry Ford said about that: "Thinking is the hardest thing a man can do, probably the reason so few of them do it."

It takes hard work to learn a great deal about something. One way schools and colleges force us to learn is through tests and grades. Be honest! Would you have sat and studied in school—I mean *really* have studied something that didn't come easily—if you weren't held accountable by exams?

You see, no one is holding us very accountable to what we learn or fail to learn as students of riding, at least not in the United States. In Germany, where it's routine for a young rider to have to endure levels of instruction complete with written, oral, and riding proficiency exams over a period of several years, it's a far different story. In the United States,

Scott, three-time National Combined Driving Single Horse Champion in 2005, 2006, and 2011, has represented the United States three times internationally at the USET level as well as once for Canada as a navigator. His horse Shadow, a Morgan, has twice been USEF Horse of the Year and once Morgan Horse of the Year.

When Scott Monroe started lap swimming in the winter months to stay fit and conditioned for competition, he brought his Morgan, Shadow, to an indoor circular pool for swim sessions as well. As Scott built up his running miles, Shadow did the same in front of the carriage.

Today, Scott enjoys a full judging and clinic schedule, as well as volunteering.

Discipline: Combined Driving

Scott has more than twenty-five years of driving and training experience. He is an ADS "R" Combined Driving Judge, ADS "r" Technical Delegate, USEF "r" Combined Driving Judge, USEF "r" Technical Delegate, a PATH Level 2 Therapeutic Driving Instructor, and most recently, an Equestrian Canada Senior Combined Driving Judge. As a PATH Instructor, Scott has a special connection with veterans as he served in the United States Marine Corps.

Life circumstances:

I started my search for the perfect horse at forty, and with no equestrian experience, my aspiration was the United States Equestrian Team. My Morgan, Shadow, entered my life as a three-year-old in 1996. He was a big-boned, soft-eyed beauty, and as green and willing as I was. I felt a connection that I could not explain and knew then we would one day be on the Team.

Hooked on horses when:

I like to think that my father's stories of his riding adventures with his horse "Thunder" as well as his car racing may have been the beginning of combined driving for me. The late Charlie Kellogg gave me a tour of his carriage collection and his horses. Something about the wheels, carriages, and those powerful black steeds pulled at my heart strings. Charlie invited me for a carriage ride soon after and that drive changed the direction of my life forever.

I think I got good because:

↪ Fitness has always been an important part of my life. I learned years ago that set training schedules can lead to soreness and boredom; I found that conditioning my horses was not any different. Rotating workouts and their duration are the key to versatility and continued interest for the horse and the man.

↪ When I started with horses many years ago, too much training was achieved by force. I knew there must be a better way and found it in natural horsemanship books and clinics. I do not want my horse to submit to me; I want him to be a willing partner.

↪ Volunteering at events held at Green Mountain Horse Association in South Woodstock, Vermont, and at Hamilton Farm in Gladstone, New Jersey, was an indispensable part of my success. I participated in everything from scribing to assisting the attending veterinarian, and I absorbed everything like a sponge.

My most important advice:

↪ A horse's greatest desire is to be safe, whether under saddle or in harness. Horses are looking for a leader—be one. Leaders give direction, assurance and controlled freedom. Be that person.

↪ Horses associate so you always want to end on a good note. You should introduce them to every life experience you can find, but always make them successful.

↪ To win takes confidence. Confidence comes from ability. Ability comes from practice. And in the end, when you reach that "blue," you will realize how important every step of the journey was. It is the journey with your horse that is the true prize, so enjoy every moment of it!

just think of the T-shirt slogan: "Last week I couldn't even spell RIDING INSTRUCTOR, but now I are one!"

The fact is that an enormous body of equestrian knowledge is just sitting out there for the learning. The question then, becomes very simple. To what extent do you choose to become a student?

Watching with an Educated Eye

A person who has an "educated eye" can look at something about which he or she is educated, and can see all manner of things that a person with an uneducated eye cannot see. This is true about almost every subject. The American humorist Will Rogers said, "Everybody's ignorant, only about different things."

After my mother's death, I hired antiques appraiser Andrew Katz to evaluate her furniture for estate purposes. I looked in one corner and saw a chair. Here is what Andrew saw: "Chair of English Chippendale period form, having a molded yoke-shaped crest rail decorated with beading above a pierced vase-shaped back splat. The upholstered slip seat is supported by a valanced seat rail and square-shaped legs with back-canted back legs…constructional and design characteristics indicate the chair frames were made circa 1770–1780…"

Another antique dealer could read this and understand it thoroughly, whereas the average person just says, "Huh?"

Picture a surgeon during an operation. He is unlikely to probe around inside the patient, turn to the nurse and ask, "Hey, nurse, what's this little thingy?"

Take the average "man on the street" and ask him to describe in great detail what he saw when a horse and rider jumped a fence. Just as the average person sees "a chair" when looking at the piece of furniture Andrew described so thoroughly, so this person is likely to say, "I saw a man on a brown horse jumping over a jump made of white wooden slats." He might call it an "obstacle" or a "hurdle" instead of a jump, and he might say "a man wearing a blue coat," but that would likely be about the extent of what he saw.

Now ask the same question of long-time USEF show-jumping coach and six-time Olympian Frank Chapot. Frank would know the type of fence—vertical, oxer, Liverpool, triple bar—about how high and wide it was, and its construction. He'd know all about the tack and bitting of the horse. He'd know a great deal about the horse, whether he appeared scopey, whether or not he jumped in good form, his general size and conformation, certainly his exact color, and perhaps even his breed.

He'd tell you whether the rider got the horse to the correct take-off point from what kind of canter, and he could tell you everything about the rider's form over the fence—hands, leg position, center of gravity, use of eyes, whether or not his knee and hip angles were appropriate for the size of the jump.

A great dressage trainer, a great reiner, a great expert in virtually any horse sport can look at a horse and rider performing in her discipline and tell you volumes about what she is seeing.

If you can't do this, you don't have an "educated eye" for your sport, and it behooves you to get one. Don't expect to find it on the shelf of your favorite tack shop. You know just where to find it—it's under the section in the *How to Ride* book that says "Study."

Become a Student of Pedigree

I'll make a bet with you. Go to any horse show or competition in America, walk up to any rider and ask this question: "What is the breeding of your horse? Who is the sire, who is the dam, and who is the sire of the dam?"

My bet is that nine out of ten of those riders won't have a clue. Not a clue. To assume that ten percent will have a clue is being generous. It's more likely not one in twenty will know anything substantial about the pedigree of the horse upon which he or she is sitting.

It's as if pedigree is entirely irrelevant, as if the traits and characteristics that the horse possesses just dropped out of the sky to magically invest that horse with all the abilities it needs to satisfy its rider's goals. But stallion breeding fees vary widely (wildly, even) for a reason. Some

"My Horse Won't Do What I Want"

At a visceral rather than intellectual level, Americans are barraged with the notion that animals feel, think, and respond like a kind of subspecies of perhaps somewhat incomplete human beings This misleading perception is termed "anthropomorphism." Early on a typical Saturday or Sunday morning, go into a house where young children live and you're likely to find the television is the babysitter, letting the parents get a little more sleep. On the screen before the transfixed gaze of the tiny tots are cartoons, full of little animals—whether mice, rabbits, bears, pigs, horses—with one thing in common: They talk, and act, like humans.

Comic books are full of similar stories. The Walt Disney Studio was founded on the premise that Mickey and Minnie and all of the creatures of the Magic Kingdom are just like us. There are books full of talking animals—*Black Beauty*, the Thornton W. Burgess series about creatures of the forest and fields—the list is endless. The effect of all these cartoons, movies, and books on their viewers and readers is to create responses to animals' actions that have nothing to do with reality. Our responses are based on wrong assumptions, but those assumptions are so deeply rooted that if you want an exercise in frustration, just try to convince someone that her horse isn't "misbehaving" on purpose.

"My horse won't do what I want!" How often have you heard this statement? But now the train of logical thinking starts to go off the track. It is true that the rider's horse isn't doing what she wants him to do. That much is a fact. But unless the rider is a true, honest-to-God, educated horseman, the conclusions stemming from the initial statement will be untrue—here's how the anthropomorphic "logic" usually works in real life:

"My horse is misbehaving."

"My horse is being bad."

"I, therefore, have permission to punish him."

In contrast, here are some possible *correct* conclusions, stemming from the premise "My horse won't do what I want":

"I must not be explaining what I want correctly."

"He must not have a base of work thorough enough to enable him, either mentally, physically, or emotionally, to perform the action that I want him to perform."

"My seat (hands, balance, whatever) is not steady and 'feeling' enough to convey the proper stimuli to induce him to perform the action that I desire."

"In making this request of my horse, I am creating athletically induced pain, either from asking him to lift more than he has been prepared to lift, or stretch more than he has been prepared to stretch. I need to go back to an easier level, build a proper foundation, then try again."

These are the right kinds of conclusions that are drawn by true trainers and real horsemen with correct knowledge of how horses experience and respond to stimuli. The wrong conclusions, that the horse is "misbehaving" and "being bad," stem from the rider's misinformed perception that the horse has a malign "motive." The rider's false premise is that the horse understands and is capable of doing what he or she wants, but simply chooses not to out of stubbornness or for other contrary reasons.

So the rider starts to get frustrated and angry. The horse gets more confused and upset. The rider gets even more frustrated and angry, and the horse gets even more confused and upset....The downward spiral has begun. It has nowhere to go but down, and it can lead to some real brutality on the part of the rider.

I don't know any rider who hasn't been guilty of this, sometime, somewhere. The good riders and good horsemen usually catch themselves before it gets out of hand. The really bad riders almost never do. That's why so many horses live their life in a world of fear, pain, and conflict—because their riders are angry people and terrible horsemen. This is the single worst part of the entire saga of man's relationship with the horse. Robert Frost wrote, "God mocked the lofty land with little men." We can modify this line to, "God mocked the lofty species with little men."

Training derived from genuine knowledge and true thinking, not false anthropomorphic thinking, is one of the most important choices you have to make if you ever expect to be a quality horseperson.

The animal shall not be measured by man. In a world older and more complete than ours, they move finished and complete, gifted with extension of the senses we have lost or never attained, living by voices we shall never hear. They are not brethren; they are not underlings; they are other nations, caught with ourselves in the net of life and time, fellow prisoners of the splendor and travail of the earth.

—Henry Beston,
The Outermost House, 1928

stallions pass on their traits consistently to foals from a variety of mares—traits that include not only conformation, but athletic talent.

It almost as if the horse world is divided into two groups of people—pedigree people, who are keenly interested in horse breeding, and a much larger group, non-pedigree people, who care nothing about their horses' antecedents, as long as their horses can get the job done.

The importance of pedigree as a predictor of future performance in Thoroughbred racing is enormous. I read an article years ago by a Fasig-Tipton Sale Company representative, whose job it was to evaluate yearlings and to decide which sales would accept those youngsters. He said something to this effect:

> Suppose three plain, bay, yearling stallions are standing in a line. All three are basically straight-legged and correct. All three move well. All three look pretty much alike. Without knowing their pedigrees, I'd be hard-pressed to give you $5,000 apiece for them.
>
> One of these colts is by a very modest stallion, out of a "nothing" mare. He's worth $5,000. The second is by a good stallion out of an allowance-producing mare, and he's probably going to fetch around $50,000. But the third colt is by Mr. Prospector out of a stakes-producing Danzig mare, and he's worth right around $500,000.

In the riding disciplines there won't be a half-million dollar disparity in the value of two young horses based solely on pedigree, but if I were looking for a jumper prospect, and I knew that he was by Corrado out of a Quidam De Revel mare, I'd be infinitely more interested in him than if he had no jumping bloodlines. It's not so difficult to study the pedigrees of the winning horses in any breed or discipline. It's available knowledge, but surprisingly, very few riders—at least in the United States—seem to take advantage of this opportunity.

The Horse: A Rowboat or a Yacht?

Realist vs. Dreamer

Mr. Spock, a character in the television series *Star Trek*, is half-human and half-Vulcan. The two halves of his personality are continually at odds because while Vulcans think logically and rationally, humans allow their thinking to be swayed by emotion.

In the world of horses, as in so many aspects of our lives, we too seem to suffer from this Vulcan versus human balancing act—often to our detriment.

We go to look at a sane, steady, reliable thirteen-year-old Quarter Horse gelding, and come home with a flighty four-year-old Thoroughbred filly because we were so taken by her grace and agility as she leapt and cavorted in the adjacent paddock. The fact that she is basically an unride-able threat to life and limb is obliterated by her transcendent beauty. The Vulcan logic was plowed under by all-too-human emotion.

So ask yourself this question: Am I basically a realist, able to ratio-nally analyze and evaluate situations as they are, or am I a dreamer, more prone to color these situations with the tints and tones of what I would like them to be?

So many of the great horsemen and horsewomen I know are able to make the hard, logical choices, not just about horse selection, but in varied aspects of their life. They neither see the world through rose-colored glasses, nor through lenses darkly distorted, but clearly, objectively and realistically.

Many of us let our emotions about horses lead us to choices that winners wouldn't make. If we accept the premise that a horse needs to be sound, sane, and athletic to achieve competitive success with any degree of consistency, then it follows logically that winners won't choose horses that are unsound or insane or unathletic. Nor will they stick with horses that might once have been sound, sane, and athletic but have become chronically unsound enough to limit their competitive use. Here's where emotion gets in the way of logical thinking.

Example One—Not Sound Enough

A friend had an endurance mare who seemed to have all the right ingredients. She was steady emotionally, didn't pull like a train for the first ten or twenty miles of a 50- or 100-mile race like so many do, and she could stay cool while other horses galloped by her. She stood quietly at holds, ate well, and her pulse dropped like a rock. She had a smooth, ground-covering trot, and a light balanced canter; she didn't forge or interfere even in bad footing, and she seemed tireless over the worst, hilliest terrain.

But after her third 100-mile race, she was lame in her left front leg, and the veterinarian diagnosed the injury as "a mild suspensory pull." My friend gave her about three months off, and then put her carefully back into work before eventually riding her very conservatively in a fairly level 50-mile race. She was lame again the next day.

The mare got another prolonged break, then another careful rehab during which time she stayed sound, but she was lame once again after a six-hour ride. In other words, this mare was just fine until the "pedal hit the metal"—but it took my friend nearly three years to finally conclude that this was not going to be the 100-mile endurance horse of her dreams.

Example Two—Not Sane Enough

In the sport of eventing, the horse and rider with the fewest overall penalty points win the competition: Penalties incurred in dressage are added to cross-country penalties, and to that score are added any show-jumping penalties. One sure way to improve your chances of doing well is to start with a good dressage score. And a sure way to make a mess of dressage is to have a hot, tense horse.

A student of mine had a gelding that was a classic Dr. Jekyll/Mr. Hyde when it came to dressage. One day he seemed steady and willing, but then on another day he was nervous and tight. What made this particular horse so frustrating was that he was a fast, brave "cross-country machine," and he was clean and accurate in show jumping.

We tried all the usual remedies. We cut his grain. We gave him hours of turnout. We longed him early in the morning before dressage to let him buck and play the "edge off." We tried a long warm up—we tried practically no warm up. Yet once the judge ran her bell for Trish to enter the arena, all bets were off.

It took Trish several years to come to the conclusion that this horse was, as the saying goes, "close, but no cigar." Those were years she could have spent developing a different horse, one that didn't have a "missing link" in his temperament.

Example Three—Not Athletic Enough

Again in eventing, there's nothing quite as endlessly frustrating as riding into the stadium—the final phase of a big event—as "leader of the pack," only to be sitting on a horse that often knocks down one, two, or multiple rails in show jumping.

A friend and former teammate of mine who is acknowledged to be one of the best event riders in the world had one of these unreliable show jumpers. The horse seemed to have a sixth sense about whether the fence was solid, or could be knocked out of the cups with impunity. He'd jump like a superstar on the cross-country course, only to lose in stadium by bringing down multiple rails.

In general, a horse that knocks three rails down is considered to have had a pretty bad round, so after James (not his real name) exited the jumping arena of a significant European event with eight rails scattered in the dirt, he climbed off that horse for the last time. The horse went on to have a decent career with a young rider at a much lower level, though even then he'd knock down rails from time to time—just to keep in practice, I guess.

As well as earning both individual gold and team silver medals at the 2004 Athens Olympics riding for Great Britain, Leslie Law contributed to many other British team triumphs, including team silver at the Sydney Olympics, team bronze at the 2002 World Equestrian Games, and team golds at several European championships.

Leslie Law and Shear L'eau at the Kentucky Three-Day Event in 2006.

Discipline: Eventing

Leslie's achievements in individual competition include repeated top-ten finishes at Burghley and Badminton (England) and the Kentucky Three-Day Event (US) four-star events, and many Advanced Level (three-star) wins on a wide range of horses. He rode for the UK in the 2018 Nations Cup and was named the US Equestrian Eventing Emerging Athlete Coach in 2014.

Life circumstances:

My family in England were typical working class. My parents didn't ride, although my father loved animals; he had a small transport business for which my mother did the secretarial work.

Hooked on horses when:

My brother Graham was the horse-crazy one at first. My parents gave in to his longings when I was about nine and bought a cheap Welsh-cross pony. We both rode it, and things developed from there, possibly because of the fraternal competition.

I think I got good because:

◔ We rode in Pony Club, which in England does a fantastic job and is a great inspiration to all young equestrians.

◔ When I left school intent on a career with horses, I worked for a large dealer's "yard" where we trained horses for amateur point-to-point races, and I absorbed a lot about good horsemanship there.

◔ I had some wonderful mentors. I was lucky to meet US jumper rider Ian Silitch during his stay in England, and he invited me to come to his barn as a working student for a couple of years when I was eighteen or nineteen. I rode young horses for Olympic eventer Ginny Leng; just being around that atmosphere and professionalism made me want to be better and better. Later, I had marvelous help with dressage from Christopher Bartle, a very bright and articulate man.

◔ We are very lucky in Britain to have strong competition and a large base of professional riders to watch and from whom to learn.

◔ Through all this I think I was impelled to keep chipping away at the goal by the kind of determination I had known in my father, who strived to make a great job of whatever he did and to see it through.

My most important advice:

First find a good mentor who has been successful and who knows what it's all about. If you're involved in a good operation it may not be the actual riding lessons you're taught, but everything that goes on around you and from which you can learn so much—the people management, the competitiveness, the production of a good horse from start to finish (which is one of my favorite things to do). Things just rub off when you ride alongside good people. Next, as well as being a good rider to be successful, you need to be mentally solid. For myself, I try not to get too down during low times and not to celebrate the highs too much. It helps to keep your feet on the ground.

Leslie Law

It's disappointing enough to have one of the big three—sound, sane, athletic—as the missing entity, but plenty of riders manage to tolerate the lack of all three at the same time, in the same horse! Read my lips: Unsound, insane, and unathletic is *not* your horse of choice! No matter how cute and fuzzy he may be.

There's a phenomenon I've often noticed in horse sports when a rider competes more than one horse. She might place first on one horse and twenty-third on another, on the same day in the same show or event.

She, of course, gets all the accolades for winning, and no blame for her "failure" on the other horse. Yet if the only horse she'd had was the twenty-third-place horse, nobody would have given her a second glance.

Here is more proof that it's mostly about the horse. This rider didn't suddenly, in the two hours between horses, get lots better or lots worse. It was the difference in the piece of "equipment"!

Winning riders have the ability to find winning horses, which includes the ability to shed themselves of losing horses, once those horses have had a fair shot and have continually come up short. This may sound cold to riders who still regard their horses as companions or pets as well as (or instead of) as "equipment"—but it's the reality.

The Horse You Choose

More than most of the hundreds of other choices that are yours to make, the horse you choose to buy is the one over which you have the greatest control. You don't have to sign that check. You don't own that horse yet; you *can* walk away.

However…one minute he's a bay horse over there; the next minute he's *your* bay horse over here. The minute you sign the check and he is yours, you invest your new horse with all your hopes and dreams. Once you've made this choice, you have to be a pretty tough cookie to say, "Oops! I goofed! I need to sell him and look at some more horses." Instead you begin to make every excuse known to man for him, and you may find parting from him next to impossible. So, try to get it right *before* you choose.

With this heads-up in mind, let's assume you are contemplating the purchase of a new horse. If you want the horse to be registered to a specific breed, or suitable for a specific discipline like reining or cutting, these are your very first requirements. Then there are a host of other qualities, characteristics and traits that differentiate bad horses from average horses, average horses from good horses, and good horses from great ones. You need to know how to evaluate all these differences if you hope to be a consistently successful rider. If you can't do this yourself, then you'd better be accompanied by someone whom you trust, and who can!

Temperament—"Oh Wow!" or "Oh No!"

Just as humans have traits of character, so do horses. There are horses with huge generosity of spirit and a willingness to try, and there are sulky, balky, obstinate creatures that pin their ears and sullenly refuse to say, "Yes," to the simplest human request.

Certainly some of this—sometimes much of this—is man-made. If the trainer is quiet, patient, systematic, caring, and knowledgeable, her chances of eliciting cooperation are greatly enhanced. However, if the so-called "trainer" is rough, aggressive, bad-tempered, inept, and impatient, she can destroy even the most potentially wonderful horse and turn it into a fearful creature of resistance.

But let's assume that you are a kind and sympathetic rider. Even so, some horses have more generosity of spirit than others. The good horses are less afraid, less flighty, less stubborn, and less likely to say, "No."

My friend David Hopper has sold hundreds of sport horses each year for more than forty years. He told me that when he's evaluating a horse's temperament, he uses a scale of one to ten. On David's scale, "a 'ten' is an unrideable maniac, and the only difference between a 'one' and a dead horse is that the 'one' eats!"

What follows are the gradations of temperament in between.

"One" to "Four" Horses Absorb Mistakes
Horses from "one" through "four" are very low-key; nothing much

bothers them. They stand still while you mount them; they don't jig and fuss at the walk. These horses don't shy at every little sound or unusual sight; they don't rear or balk or buck or bolt. You can bounce around on them and they just keep plugging along. Your hands can be erratic, and they don't fling their head all over the place. Essentially, the horses with temperaments "one" through "four" *absorb* their rider's mistakes.

Very timid riders should ride a "one," "two," or "three." These horses will never intimidate them by running away. On the contrary, getting them out of a walk is usually more of a problem! As the rider's confidence increases, the level of horse can rise accordingly.

"Five" and "Six" Horses *Tolerate* Mistakes

"Fives" and "sixes" put up with their rider's mistakes, within reason. These horses are in great demand because they have enough spark to be dashing in competition, but not so much spark that they are constantly at risk of bursting into flame. Many good riders, even those capable of riding "sevens" and even "eights," always seek out the solid comfort coupled with the get-up-and-go that the "five" and "six" horses provide.

"Sevens" and Higher *Magnify* Mistakes

Horses with temperaments of "seven" and higher tend to exaggerate their rider's mistakes. They feel the rider lurching around and they get nervous and start to spook or jig or get flighty. Only riders with extreme tact and good control over their own body parts make it look easy to ride "sevens" and "eights." (Forget "nines" and "tens"; they just are not suitable riding horses.)

I know several great riders who prefer these higher-octane horses. I guess, for them, it's like driving a Ferrari. They know how to get along with this level of nervous energy, they are comfortable doing so, and they like the adrenaline rush.

Much of the distress in the horse world, from the rider's perspective and from the horse's, comes about because a rider, who should be riding a "four" or a "five" is inexpertly attempting to deal with a "seven" or an "eight."

Soundness—Whatever *That* Means

There is much that soundness is, and there's also much that soundness is not, and many a wonderful horse is lost because neither the rider nor the veterinarian can deal with the nuances of these differences.

To some people, sound means not lame, not sick, and not bedeviled by various vices like cribbing, weaving, or other neurotic behaviors.

To some veterinarians doing pre-purchase exams, soundness is all of the above, plus the absence of significant abnormalities in X-rays, plus the absence of any major conformational flaws that might some day lead to physical unsoundness.

But is it really that simple?

Let's say you are competing at some huge, four-star event like olex or Badminton, just about the toughest test that you can ask a horse to do. The horse you're sitting on has been operated on for pharyngeal paralysis (roaring). He has significant navicular changes in both front hooves, plus some arthritic changes in both hocks. He has a big wire-cut scar on his left hind pastern. He toes in on both forefeet, more noticeably on the left fore. He has a grade-one heart murmur. He's a cribber.

This horse would have about as much chance of passing a conventional pre-purchase exam as a cow would have outrunning a cheetah. But he performs a lovely, elegant dressage test, powers around one of the toughest, most massive cross-country courses in the world, passes the Sunday morning jog with flying colors, jumps clear over a four-foot, three-inch stadium course, and ends up in the top three on the victory podium.

So is this horse sound? Or unsound?

This whole sound/unsound question has few easy answers. There are too many tradeoffs and shades of gray once you get past the obvious "blacks" (lame, with a fractured coffin bone) at one end of the soundness curve and the "whites" (sound, with virtually perfect X-rays) at the other. You, as an individual, with your particular goals in mind and in consultation with experienced veterinarians, will need to choose how much risk with which you are comfortable.

Fig. 20 Jumper riders use the word "scope" to describe the sheer power a horse must possess to jump up and over a fence that is both high and wide. Here, King Oscar is about to take off over an uphill bounce jump on the old Advanced course at Millbrook, New York, back in the early 1990s. You can see how he's coiled to spring, much as your cat crouches before she leaps up onto your kitchen counter!

Athleticism: Is He a Cat or a Cow?

If you're anywhere near my age, you may remember the grade-school, gym-period ordeal of being "picked for the team." Two team captains appointed for whatever the game was to be took turns choosing members for their team until only a downcast klutz who could never seem to catch a softball was left to be reluctantly absorbed by the last team to choose.

Don't fall in love with the equine equivalent of the last kid to get picked! Instead, ask yourself before you drive to the seller's farm what your reason is for buying a horse. Are you looking primarily for an expensive pet, or for an essential piece of athletic "equipment"?

Once you resolve to choose an athletic horse (fig. 20), there remain huge variables under the general heading "athleticism" because of the question that looms large: "Athletic for what?"

Secretariat may have been the most athletic horse to hit the racetrack in the last fifty years, but he probably would have been hopelessly inept as a reiner, a cutter, a dressage horse, or a five-gaited show horse.

Each riding sport or discipline has its own set of standards and challenges, and each prospective horse must be measured against these requirements. This means that you have to be thoroughly educated and knowledgeable about what it is your sport is testing.

You may need a crystal ball even if you know what you'd like to have in a horse, because unless the horse you are evaluating already knows how to perform in your sport, many of the requisite athletic qualities aren't readily apparent. For all that you can see, there are athletic qualities that you won't even be able to look for until you get to a certain level of competition, and you may be cruelly disappointed not to see them when you get there.

Suppose you are considering a two-year-old as a potential cutting horse. He may appear nimble and swift, but you don't know if he has that "cow" instinct that will make the difference.

Maybe you're looking at a six-year-old Arabian endurance prospect. He appears to have it all: He's light on his feet, balanced, and agile; he has a fast, powerful, sweeping trot and a ground-covering canter so soft you can scarcely hear his feet hit the ground. But as for the sheer toughness and the ability—when he is fit—to carry these gaits up over Squaw Peak and down through the jumbled boulders of the Granite Chief Wilderness on the Tevis Cup, these are qualities you simply cannot see—at least, not yet.

A young dressage prospect may blow you away with his brilliant, lofty gaits. You don't know whether, after some years of correct training, those athletic qualities you see so clearly now will translate into the ability to perform passage, piaffe, and tempi-changes.

Sometimes we get it right, but even the greatest horsemen sometimes read it wrong. Think of the Keeneland (Kentucky) and Saratoga (New York) Yearling Sales, where every summer the sharpest horsemen in racing spend *millions* on untried babies—most of which never win enough on the track to pay back their purchase prices. When you strike it rich in sizing up a horse it's partly blind, dumb luck, even though you'll want to call it superior judgment!

Louise has been champion at every major show on the East Coast, riding horses whose names—Harbor Bay, Irresistible, Catch a Spark, Red Panda, Gray Slipper—sound like a hunter/jumper world who's who. She was Leading Hunter Rider at the 2008 Pennsylvania National and received the Old Springhouse Lifetime Achievement Award at the 2009 Capital Challenge. She is a co-founder of the American Hunter Jumper Foundation (AHJF) and was inducted into the National Show Hunter Hall of Fame in 2012.

Louise Serio on Ocean Park in the first ever World Cup Team Hunter Challenge, Las Vegas, Nevada, 2005.

Discipline: Hunter/Jumper

In addition to winning the World Champion Hunter Rider (WCHR) National Championship twice (in 2001 and 2005), Louise was a member of the 2007 US team *that defeated the European team at the WCHR World Cup Team Hunter Challenge in Las Vegas. Riding Castle Rock, she won the $50,000 Chronicle of the Horse/US Hunter Jumper Association (USHJA) International Hunter Derby in 2010.*

Life circumstances:

My mother, Mary Warner Brown, taught riding for a living; lessons at her barn Derbydown in Chester County, Pennsylvania, cost five dollars an hour. She had attended a college with an equestrian program and read the books by Captain Vladimir Littauer and the other greats. She taught the basics. She didn't make us kids ride; it just happened: My older sister and I came home from school and rode. There wasn't a lot of television-watching in that era.

Hooked on horses when:

It wasn't a big decision, I just didn't veer off the path that began while I was growing up. It never occurred to me to do something else.

I think I got good because:

↪ My childhood was a lot of very easy times with ponies and horses, a lot of play and a lot of learning, too. Derbydown had a small pony program and if we needed a pony we'd go out in the field and break another one and off we'd go. Whenever we were "just riding," though, my mother was always teaching someone. I can hear her and her instruction in my mind, from all those years.

↪ I did my share of winning as a junior but my sister Mary was the child star, winning Best Child Rider at Devon among other things. But I think never winning at the level like she did made me want to win a little bit more. And I think because I wasn't as serious about it when I was young, I've been able to keep going in the sport longer.

↪ I've been blessed with wonderful horses.

My most important advice:

↪ Be sympathetic to your horse and make sure your goals and your horse's fit together. By that I mean, make sure he's equipped to do the best he can: his mental status, his ability, his soundness. Keep all that in mind and understand that if he's not doing as well as he might, there may be a reason for that. You need to communicate with him about what's right and what's wrong for him.

↪ If you participate in a sport and enjoy its benefits, consider giving back your time and energy—and your opinion—to help make it better. Once you get involved in something like the AHJF, it opens up new worlds.

Are Horse Buyers Liars?

There's an old real-estate expression, "Buyers are liars." Trudy Abbott, a real-estate broker in Norwich, Vermont, shared that with me forty years ago. She went on to describe how people who told her they wanted a house in a village would end up buying a remote one-hundred-acre farm, or they would say they wanted a waterfront property, then purchase a ski lodge. "I don't think they're really liars," Trudy explained. "I think they just don't know what they want."

It's so often the same in the horse business. A prospective purchaser comes specifically to look at an eight-year-old gelding, but falls in love with a four-year-old filly. Or she buys a small horse when she wanted a big one, or buys a bay when she specifically wanted a gray. There is often not a lot of rhyme or reason (at least none that is readily apparent) in the decision-making process, because the buyer has not really decided what she wants, or why.

We humans are so easily led by our emotions more than by our logic that we need to take a look at this process of buying on a whim, because it can wreak such havoc in our quest to become really good riders. So ask yourself these two simple questions.

1   Do I actually want to become a good rider, or am I just playing around?
2   If I do want to get good, is this a horse that will help make that happen?

Once you decide what you really want in a horse—perhaps it's more accurate to say what you really *need* in a horse—then you are faced with how to afford it.

It's impossible to talk about acquiring the right horse without talking about money, because usually the most successful winners, if they are for sale at all, cost the most money.

For some people, money isn't really the problem. Some of the richest men and women in the world either own and ride really good horses, or own good horses and pay others to ride them. So when these people go horse shopping, they don't have to make any compromises. If a successful event horse needs to have lovely gaits, a big jump, a wonderful temperament, and also must be sound, bold, fast, and tough, the "deep pockets" buyers will look only at the horses in which all of these qualities are readily apparent. When a seller trots out a horse and the wealthy buyer doesn't like the way the horse moves, that horse just goes right back into his stall. The buyer won't even sit in the saddle.

But the majority of riders, those without an unlimited budget, need to figure out which compromises they're willing to make.

Suppose I'm looking for an event horse that might someday jump around the Rolex Kentucky Three-Day Event. Assuming that the ideal upper-level eventer I just described is out of my price range, there are lots of possible compromises that could bring a horse's price down to a level where I can actually bring him home.

◆ Ideally I'd like a horse between six and nine years old and 16.1 to 16.3 hands high. But maybe something four years old and 15.3 hands will cost less.

◆ I've found a horse I like and he is very sound. But he's eleven years old, not eight or nine.

◆ I want a beautiful mover. But at the trot, this horse is only a good mover.

◆ I'd like a spectacular jumper. But although the horse I can afford is a scopey jumper, he doesn't jump in great form and hangs his knees a bit.

◆ I'd like my new horse to be calm and quiet. But I've found a prospect in my price range that is a bit hot, or green, or "race-tracky."

◆ Ideally, I want a bay gelding. But this is a chestnut mare.

◆ I love Thoroughbreds. But this horse is part Thoroughbred and part Appaloosa.

Fig. 21 New Zealander Mark Todd, seen here riding the stallion Aberjack at the Blarney Castle event in Ireland, reached the summit of the Mount Everest of the riding world when the Fédération Equéstre Internationale (FEI) named him "Horseman of the Century." Only one of us in each one hundred years can pull that off, but that's no reason not to try to be the Sir Edmund Hillary of your breed or sport.

Let's be real. It's a whole lot easier when we don't have to compromise. On the other hand, the world is full of success stories about compromises that worked.

■ Success Stories

New Zealand's famous (and very tall) eventer Mark Todd, FEI "Horseman of the Century," drove quite a long way in 1983 to look at Charisma when he was offered the ride on the gelding while his top horse was laid up (fig. 21). He was surprised to discover that the prospect he'd traveled so far to see was a pudgy and unprepossessing 15.3 hands. Two Olympic gold medals later, Mark had got over the shock, and he and Charisma were a legendary partnership.

Ben O'Meara didn't get Untouchable off the racetrack until the horse was eleven years old, an age at which most riders would have written him off. But Untouchable became one of the great Olympic Grand Prix jumpers.

Despite being an already *"Wow!"* jumper, Theodore O'Connor, an Arab/Shetland/Thoroughbred-mix just shy of 14.2 hands, was anything but my impression of a four-star horse when Christan Trainor brought him to my farm as a four-year-old. But Karen O'Connor saw something special in him a year later, and after finishing third at Rolex Kentucky in 2007, they won both team and individual gold at the Pan Am Games. (Teddy was short-listed for the 2008 Olympics when he died as a result of a freak farm accident.)

Victor Dakin wasn't the prototype of my ideal eventer when I went to look at him in 1973. He was barely sixteen hands, his feet were narrow, his pasterns upright. He was hot as a firecracker to ride in dressage, and the Canadian Team coach had dismissed him, stating, "This bloody horse can't canter!" He was one-half Thoroughbred, one-quarter Irish Draught, one-eighth Arabian, and one-eighth Morgan—hardly the usual mix for a top eventing prospect.

But he could run and jump forever.

By choosing to "compromise" on Victor, I was able to ride on a gold-medal-winning USET team, win the US National Championship, and ride clear rounds on cross-country over most of the world's toughest courses for five consecutive seasons (fig. 22).

Victor is a good example of a compromise that was a good choice, but I have also made my share of mistakes. I think many of the times I've made horse-buying mistakes it's because I wanted to get something for nothing—or, to put it in plain English, because I'm cheap! I wanted to buy champagne, but I had a beer pocketbook, so I'd often get a horse that had some problem, rather than pay several times as much for a better horse.

By "problem," I mean I would frequently buy horses that were hard to ride, either too hot or too strong, or very green. Always, of course, I'd do so assuming that I could fix that horse's particular problems, and that often proved to be a wrong assumption. Hot horses tend to stay hot, and tough, aggressive horses sometimes calm down, but more often they don't. Green is fixable; it just takes time.

But my worst buying mistakes happened when I would compromise *quality*, a word that means different things to different horsemen, even when they are in the same discipline—and especially when they are in different disciplines.

Fig. 22 Victor Dakin was a cross-country machine. Barely 16 hands, he was one-half Thoroughbred, one-quarter Irish Draught, one-eighth Morgan, and one-eighth Arabian. His eventing career lasted almost 20 years, and at one point he went about five years at the Advanced level without a cross-country jumping fault. Here, at the 1976 Olympic selection trials in Middletown, Delaware, he makes his big leap look like a Pony Club fence.

In eventing, horses with "quality" are fancy movers. They trot with an elastic "flow," and their canter is buoyant and uphill. Their gallop is silky and reaching, their jump is sharp and full of scope and power. If you start with a horse full of quality, you have realistic hopes. But if you compromise basic quality, you'll never get there—no matter how much you struggle, and no matter how much riding skill you bring to the equation.

Breeds

If you are only interested in one specific breed, and expect to compete mainly against other horses of that same breed, you are obviously restricted in your horse search to those horses with registration papers in your breed of choice.

Every breed has a standard of conformation, a sort of idealized prototype of how the perfect horse is meant to look. As a prospective purchaser you will want to consider that. Having done so, you are right back to all the considerations like soundness, temperament, and athleticism that hold true for any other horse.

A breed is a group of horses with shared ancestors, usually in a breed registry. Most breeds have a long recorded history that explains why and how the breed was created and what its greatest strengths have historically been. This is like a little thumbnail sketch encapsulating the essence of the breed.

"The Arabian, 'drinkers of the wind,' a creature of the desert, beautiful and hardy, who shared his master's tent."

"The Morgan, the tough yet gentle companion of the pioneers, whose versatility helped forge a new nation."

"The Quarter Horse, the strong, agile and gentle horse of choice of the Western cowboy, great with cattle and all manner of ranch chores."

"The American Saddlebred, stylish, flashy, elegant, the 'peacock of the horse world.'"

And so on. Each breed devotee will have a hundred reasons why their chosen breed exceeds all others in desirability.

In contrast, there are disciplines such as reining, cutting, eventing, foxhunting, dressage, show hunters, and jumpers that are theoretically

Eighteen Horses—Fifty-Seven Years

I've bought and sold hundreds of horses since the day my parents bought me Paint when I was ten years old, and I've probably ridden thousands.

I've chosen just eighteen of them to tell a tale of trial, error, and adventure, in the hopes that it may give some insight into what sometimes works and sometimes doesn't—maybe even some insight about what constitutes a wise choice.

Paint was a stroke of pure luck, the perfect first pony for a little boy. He was tolerant and kind; he could run fast enough to satisfy my yen for cowboying; he didn't jig, and I could ride him with or without a saddle or bridle. He gave me enormous confidence, and by the time I was thirteen, he had made me think that I was already a great rider.

My second horse, **Bonfire**, probably a Quarter Horse of some sort, was a "Steady Eddie" like Paint. He was also tough enough and game enough to let me attain my first major riding goal: completion of the 1956 Green Mountain Horse Association 100-Mile Competitive Trail Ride.

Lippitt Sandy, my third horse, was a Morgan with all that breed's versatility, allowing me to sample several horse sports. I rode him in two GMHA 100-Mile rides and competed on him at the National Morgan Horse Show in Northampton, Massachusetts. I drove him hitched to a sulky in a half-mile harness race, and he pulled a stone boat in the Justin Morgan Memorial class.

A few years and many Morgans later, after I'd seen my first three-day event in 1961 and become instantaneously addicted, I bought my first Thoroughbred. **Lighting Magic** was a bay, five-year-old gelding, nick-named "Dennis" (confusing, I know). Dennis took me around my first three-day event at GMHA in 1962, then around my first Intermediate-level three-day event in 1965. I raced him over fences, showed him in hunter classes at the Ox Ridge Horse Show, and hunted him many long hours with the Essex Foxhounds in New Jersey. He was the prototypical all-around horse, just not quite a scopey-enough jumper for the huge demands of Advanced-level eventing.

I bought a big, rawboned, gray gelding of unknown breeding named **Cat** in the late 1960s. He'd supposedly been a barrel racer in Oklahoma, he was spooky and quirky—but if there was one thing Cat could do, it

Fig. 23 Nothing back in the United States had prepared me for the size and complexity of the cross-country course at the 1974 World Championship at Burghley (England). Here, Victor Dakin leaps out over the Waterloo Rails, with its six-and-one-half foot drop. Perhaps what I lacked in experience and skill, I made up with determination and drive, and obviously, Victor's huge ability to jump clean. We were one of fifteen clear cross-country rounds out of sixty that day. But over the years since that gold medal weekend, I've realized that I mainly learned to ride *after* winning that medal.

was jump. He became my first Advanced three-day horse at the 1971 Dunham, Quebec, Horse Trials, and I also jumped him over a six-foot vertical fence in a jumper class at a horse show.

Then, in 1973, came the horse that dreams are made of: **Victor Dakin** (fig. 23). Gold-medal horses change your life, and Victor changed mine (see The Victor Dakin Opportunity, p. 189).

York, a brilliant New Zealand superstar I bought in 1976 at the advice and urging of my friend Lockie Richards, was the only horse I've bought sight unseen. York was deathly sick for almost two years, until surgery disclosed he was riddled with parasites that were seemingly immune to the worming procedures of that era. Finally well again, York won the 1979 US National Three-Day-Event Championships at Chesterland in Pennsylvania, and also was the US Eventing Association's 1979 Horse of the Year. He may have been the most innately brilliant horse I've ever competed.

Farnley Rob Roy was one of the few horses I rode over the years that I didn't actually own. Like Cat, Robby was a big, gray, rawboned jumping machine, loaned to me by his breeders, Matthew and Winkie Mackay-Smith. In four big international three-day events, Robbie never had a jumping fault. I felt as if I could jump him through a flaming hoop.

Core Buff, a yearling Thoroughbred stallion I bought, with his dam, Royal Core, in the early 1970s, was my first foray into event-horse breeding. I rode him and later his daughter, **Chestry Oak**, to the Advanced Level. They were possibly the only sire-daughter combination to jump around the Rolex Kentucky Three-Day Event, several years apart.

I was first smitten by **Epic Win**, another Thoroughbred stallion, when I saw him being ridden by Nancy Murray, his owner, at a clinic in Ft. Collins, Colorado. I was able to buy him a couple of years later. Epic took me around the Advanced track at Rolex a couple of times in the early 1990s, and he and I won the Bromont, Quebec, CCI Three-Day Event in 1992, shortly before my fifty-second birthday.

In 1998, I placed second in the GMHA 100-Mile Trail Ride on **Wintry Oak**, a Thoroughbred stallion by Epic Win and out of Chestry Oak. Wintry was a tough, athletic mixture of five horses I'd owned and used in my breeding program—Chee Oaks, Chestry Oak, Royal Core, Core Buff, and Epic Win. I also won a number of Preliminary-level events with Wintry, and even today, there's a son of his on our farm.

Speed Axcel was a tough, hot Thoroughbred mare. She was little, but when I jumped her I felt as if I were being propelled into space! She became my last Advanced event horse when I rode her around the Groton House Horse Trials in Massachusetts in June of 1999, just a couple of months before my fifty-eighth birthday. My Advanced eventing career had lasted for twenty-nine seasons.

In 2001, I was on a horse-buying trip in Ireland for some clients from New Jersey, when I first saw **Loftus Fox**. I bought him as a sixtieth birthday present to myself, and for the last eight years I've been competing him at Preliminary level. He has the talent to go Advanced, but at this point in my life, Preliminary looks just about right to me! In May, I rode him around the Preliminary course at Hitching Post Farm in Vermont, marking the forty-eighth consecutive season I've ridden at that level or higher.

Rett Butler was a tiny, (fifteen-hand) Arabian gelding that I bought in California in 2002. He wasn't fancy but he was totally reliable and tough as nails. When I was competing in the GMHA 100-Mile Rides in the 1950s, word had come filtering back (filtering slowly in those pre-Internet days) of an endurance race in California called the Tevis Cup that was first run in 1955. My friend, Allen Leslie had completed the race

in 1967, and I'd always felt that there was a piece missing from my riding resume—the fact that I'd never won a Tevis buckle by completing that ride within twenty-four hours, by clawing up and down those unrelenting mountains and canyons. Rett fulfilled that dream for me in 2004, at 4:13 A.M., after twenty-one hours in the saddle, probably the most dramatic adventure in all my riding years.

Now it's 2011, and I have a new event horse in the stable with Lofty, a gray off-the-track Thoroughbred called **Union Station** (fig. 24). I also have a six-year-old Warmblood gelding, **Beaulieu's Cool Skybreaker**, and a five-year-old Warmblood filly, **Beaulieu's Cool Attitude**, both from jumper lines (grandson and granddaughter of **Quidam De Revel**, they're naturally airborne and jump in classic form with their knees under their chin). And so the saga continues—as I hope it will for quite some time.

Fig. 24 The great baseball star, Satchel Paige, said, "Never look back. Something might be gaining on you!" Here in 2009, fifty-seven years after I got little Paint, I'm still trying not to look back. But I'm pretty sure they're gaining! This is Union Station competing at GMHA.

In 2002, Peter won the individual bronze medal at the World Equestrian Games in Jerez, Spain, with the Holsteiner mare Fein Cera, who was awarded the Best Horse in the Final title. Two years later, he and Fein Cera helped win a team gold medal for the United States at the Athens Olympics.

Peter Wylde on Fein Cera during the Olympic Games in Athens, Greece, 2004.

Discipline: Show Jumping

Winner of the ASPCA Maclay Equitation Finals as a junior, Peter started his own horse business after college, then relocated in the mid-1990s to Europe, becoming highly successful on the European circuit. In addition to his long partnership with Fein Cera, he had big wins with Macanuda DeNiro, Pinnochio, Quo Vadis, and many others. He is currently based at M & W, LLC, in Millbrook, New York.

Life circumstances:

I was born in the Boston, Massachusetts, area and my family wasn't horsey. When my older brother didn't like the riding lessons my parents offered him at the stable right across the street, I wasn't offered lessons until I started asking for them.

Hooked on horses when:

Our next-door neighbors had horses, and from age seven I used to go over and ride with them just for fun. I convinced my parents to get a pony when I was nine and started showing around then. I was a freak! I got up at three in the morning on Saturdays to braid my pony, pack the trailer and get everything ready before waking my parents at five-thirty to drive me to the show. We were always the first on the grounds.

I think I got good because:

🐴 I have always been very "head down, eyes forward" when it comes to riding. I was really focused on it all through elementary and high school and missed out on ski trips and parties because I was always going to a horse show.

🐴 I learned great basics as a junior from riding with Fran and Joe Dotoli and from watching and emulating top US riders like Joe Fargis.

🐴 My 1994 decision to go to Europe and ride for Swiss dealer Gerhard Etter catapulted me forward. My fellow riders at his stable were Danny Etter (who won the first two European World Cups in 2009), Cameron Hanley (who was fourth in the 2009 European Championships), and Mandy Porter, who came back to the United States and had a very successful Grand Prix career. We were great friends but also very competitive and driven to succeed. I rode eight to ten horses a day and showed four horses almost every weekend. I had good results at international shows during those years and rode on my first Nations Cup teams for the United States.

My most important advice:

Even if you get knocked down, pick yourself up and keep trying to be the best you can despite the odds. Get yourself around people who are really good at what they do, whatever the discipline. When it's time for you to take a full time job, seek out a place where you can ride a lot and show, if possible. Finally, choose a top rider whose physiognomy is similar to yours and watch everything he does, then apply his riding to your own! You can actually teach yourself that way.

Peter Wylde

open to all breeds, although some breeds are more suited to certain disciplines than others.

I've never seen a five-gaited Quarter Horse, for example. And there aren't many Hanoverians in the cutting arenas.

So once you've restricted yourself to a certain breed, you have partially restricted yourself to disciplines that you can do, and some you probably can't do.

Suppose you love the Morgan breed, but are also entranced with the sport of dressage. Certainly Morgans can be used in the discipline, but very few of them are suited for the demands of upper-level dressage, a world dominated by such Warmblood breeds as Hanoverians and Westphalians. So you'll have to choose: Buy a Morgan, and probably restrict yourself from the upper reaches of dressage, or buy a Warmblood and give yourself more of a chance to excel in your sport. (Or win the lottery and buy one of each!)

Intangibles

Whenever horsemen talk about their favorite horses, they tend to do so in terms that defy logical tangible analysis. They use the famous phrase "the look of eagles," or they say, "That mare has a lot of heart." They might praise another horse with the words, "That colt has a lot of 'try' in him," or "He'll give you everything he's got."

These are pretty hard qualities for a prospective buyer to recognize or to pin down when someone leads a bay gelding out of the barn and stands him up in the dooryard for inspection.

Yet so often it's these intangible qualities that absolutely pluck a particular horse out of the herd and make him the one you remember years later, with special respect and affection.

I wish I could say how someone might develop this almost mystical sixth sense, but apart from spending enormous amounts of time immersed with large numbers of horses (it's that ten thousand hours again, folks!), I don't think there's a formula for acquiring that rare perception.

But I do believe there are a few people who really can perceive the imperceptible.

Too Bad vs. Too Good Horses

■ Too Bad

It's inevitable that sooner or later most of us who ride come up against horses that have the potential to cause us real physical harm. The easiest, quietest horse in the world can stumble or spook with bad consequences, but these aren't the horses I'm talking about here.

I'm talking about the ones that are dangerous to get on, because they are very green, or very spooky, or very rank, or they have solidly confirmed vices like bucking and rearing.

Let's start with very green, because every horse is very green at some point in his life. There are ways to make horses un-green that are quiet and gentle and systematic, and certainly there's the old cowboy "buck 'em out" as the other extreme. But even if we do everything right, "greenies" are still much more likely to spin, or wheel, or shy, or buck, or rear, just because being ridden is such an unfamiliar feeling to them.

So then, this choice: Am I going to be the rider who brings on greenies, or am I going to let someone else do that phase of the training, and I'll take over the reins once that initial stage seems safely in the past?

This choice depends upon how brave you are, how physically fit, how experienced, how knowledgeable, how old; it depends upon lots of things.

I have two broken hips, courtesy of two buckers that I shouldn't have tried to train, because I was in my fifties for the first one, and in my sixties for the second. (I guess another way to evaluate whether or not to break babies is to calculate how stupid you are.)

Although most green horses become nice horses, some stay bad news, whether because of pain issues, or deep-seated fear issues, or maybe just because of plain old bad temper or stubborn intransigence.

It's easy to blame the horse when the rider is the problem, but sometimes it *is* the horse, which is why even the most gifted trainers give up on some horses, some of the time.

Some horses are born *spooky*. We had a mare that could buck you off if you crinkled a candy wrapper while on her back. Others hear a bird chirp, or see a chipmunk dart, and spin so fast you don't have a chance.

Worse than spooky are horses who will suddenly "go to bucking." These don't just whirl and be done with it; they whirl, get you loose, then buck you into outer space. Other horses get only so far from the barn, then stop and rear. And rear. And rear…sometimes straight up and over on top of you.

When we come up head to head with one of these problems, we have the choice to try to work through it, or send the horse to someone who specializes in problem horses, or give up on the horse altogether. It's no easy choice, but it is one place where having some common sense can save you a great deal of grief, and it can maybe save you much more than that.

◼ Too Good

At the opposite end of the spectrum are horses that present such a low degree of challenge that the rider's powers are insufficiently "stretched."

It's lulling and soothing to have horses that don't have issues, and I'd far rather have an easy horse than a tough, intractable one. That said, I think riders get better when they are challenged to ride better. Lest what I've said sounds utterly simplistic, what I mean is that I believe in the saying, "Horses 'go' as we ride them."

I believe what that maxim implies is that we get our finest results when we have honed our riding skills to a fine edge, and the horses we ride become "in tune" with our heightened skills.

Some horses, the classic Steady Eddies that are perfect for riders still learning the basic skills, may actually hold back riders who are ready for more challenge. These utterly "bombproof" horses go pretty well whether ridden by a fair rider, a good rider, or an excellent rider. This can lead the fair-to-good rider to the delusion that she is that excellent rider.

We need to sit on horses that go adequately for adequate riders, but only grant their finest gifts to riders whose gifts match their own. Don't let yourself be lulled into complacency by the too-easy-ride.

A Quiver Full of Arrows

Areas of Choice

For the sake of simplicity I encapsulated all the choices that will have a direct impact on whether you become a good—maybe even great—rider into just seven broad "Areas of Choice." To recap, these include your horse sport; your life circumstances; your support network; your character; your body; your knowledge; and your horse.

I've acknowledged that you have no control whatsoever over some things about yourself (like your age), but that you *can* change many other personal attributes, such as your physical fitness or your knowledge of a particular subject, if you're willing to bear down and do the work. Still others—like the horse you decide to buy—require that you choose to operate on analytical, disciplined thinking rather than emotion.

There are thousands of these choices! Where you live, whether or not you have instruction, how far you want to go in your sport…and some choices are so difficult that instead of choosing, certain people just waffle, only to end up unhappy with the outcome.

If the whole concept of choices starts to seem a little abstract, here's another way to think about what you are trying to do. Are you a *Lord of the Rings* fan? If so, bring to mind the Elven prince Legolas Greenleaf wielding his bow in the defense of Helm's Deep: He reaches to his quiver for arrow after arrow without even glancing back, knowing that the arrow will be there because he has filled the quiver.

I'll bet that in every equestrian discipline, if you analyzed it, you would find that the best people have the horseman's equivalent of a very full "quiver." They have the emotional and character traits that help them in their quest, they've built a support network, they live in the right places, they've developed good physical skills, and they know a lot—about pedigree, about vet issues and soundness, about conditioning, and so on. They have those pieces—those "arrows"—at hand when they need them.

What constitutes a quiver full of arrows for a top show jumper? For an eventer? An endurance rider? A reiner? It's not just the simple physical skills; it's the entire array of attributes that results from choice after choice in each of the seven categories. When you need a particular arrow, and you metaphorically reach back over your shoulder to pull it out of your quiver—as Legolas does when the Orcs are coming—it had better be there!

To have that arrow in your quiver, in other words, is very often the result of a conscious choice to put it there. It's a little like the conscious choice and effort involved in conditioning your horse for a competition. (I was trying to explain the whole conditioning concept to a bunch of California Pony Clubbers and a little boy piped up, "I get it! A horse is like a Coke machine: You've got to put the fifty cents in before you can get the Coke out!")

Reach for It, and It's There

If I'm an event rider galloping down a long hill toward an imposing jump and I feel my horse getting all strung out and on his forehand, I need to possess the skill to rebalance him and get his hocks back under him, so that my horse doesn't crash into the fence and do a terrible, cart-wheeling somersault.

When I reach into my quiver for that rebalancing skill, I want that arrow to be there!

Every riding and driving discipline for every horse breed has "arrows" that are specific to that discipline and breed. There are also arrows that are common to all horses and all styles of riding.

These may be specific physical skills; they may be character traits or emotional characteristics. When you're trying to move up in your sport, a good horse is a variant of arrow, and so is a good support network. Another arrow in your theoretical quiver might be a certain item of knowledge: It could be how to adjust a certain piece of tack or harness— or it might be factual information you've learned about Quarter Horse pedigrees to help you select one bay yearling filly over another, superficially similar, bay yearling filly.

Every one of the seven Areas of Choice listed in the previous chapters contains hundreds and hundreds of arrows that you might choose to stuff in your personal quiver.

One way to perform a checklist of where you stand would be to try to determine what arrows are the personal possessions of the top five or ten riders or drivers or trainers in your specific sport, breed, or discipline, and then compare what they have to what you have.

Here's just one example: I recently got emails with links to the Web sites of two natural horsemanship clinicians who are about to set out on national clinic and demonstration tours. When top experts have high quality Web sites, and you don't, that tells you something right there.

If you watch a major Grand Prix jumping competition, notice how few riders miss their distances to the correct take-off spots, and compare those performances to your own. If you are a "Deadeye Dick" who gets in right almost infallibly, then that's not a missing arrow for you. However, if (unlike the top riders) you flounder to find the correct distance, the contrast should tell you something.

The point is that those arrows don't just show up in the quiver by magic. Just as an actual arrowsmith crafts an individual arrow by choosing the shaft, the point, and the feathers, and by painstakingly assembling the pieces into the finished product, so a good rider has chosen and crafted the hundreds of pieces that together make a "good rider."

How to Make Your Own Luck

Sometimes you need to be ready to take aim with arrows from your quiver at something good, an opportunity that will get away if you're not prepared for it. For instance, there's that Karen O'Connor saying I love to quote: "Luck is when preparedness meets opportunity." What does it really mean in practical terms? No one knows for sure where or how, or even *whether* opportunity will arrive, so that second "half" of the equation—opportunity—doesn't come with any guarantees.

The only thing that each of us can guarantee is that we are prepared to take advantage of those opportunities if they happen to come our way. Even when opportunity doesn't drop out of the sky into our lap as a stroke of "luck" and we have to "force" the opportunity to happen, we still need to be ready. In other words, the preparedness part—the quiver full of arrows—is up to us.

The US Air Force pilot General Chuck Yeager, like legendary baseball player Ted Williams (see my treasured anecdote about him on p. 133), achieved the very pinnacle of his chosen profession. He was a triple ace as a World War II fighter plane pilot. Later, he was the first pilot in history to fly faster than the speed of sound. By all measures, he was one of the best. These are his words:

> *I have flown in just about everything, with all kinds of pilots in all parts of the world—British, French, Pakistani, Iranian, Japanese, Chinese—and there wasn't a dime's worth of difference between any of them except for one unchanging, certain fact: The best, most skillful pilot had the most experience. The more experienced, the better he is. Or, for that matter, she is.*

Ted Williams, Chuck Yeager, Mike Plumb, Bill Gates—those who have been at the summit of their chosen field, have almost all spent a minimum of ten thousand hours in their pursuits. This is the amount of time that Malcolm Gladwell's book *Outliers: The Story of Success* postulates is needed for mastery of any kind of cognitively complex field. That's twenty hours a week for ten years, or one hour a day for twenty-seven years. Ten thousand hours is an enormous amount of time to devote to something, but, to repeat, just as General Yeager said, "the best, most skillful pilot had the most experience."

You can substitute the word "rider" for the word "pilot," and the formula remains the same.

If we go back to Malcolm Gladwell's ten-thousand-hour rule, it becomes pretty obvious that what Karen O'Connor calls "preparedness" is actually nothing more than being deep into that first ten thousand hours, which means that each one of us aiming for the top of our riding discipline needs to climb aboard a horse, any horse, absolutely as often as we can find or create the chance to do so, so that we've stacked up hours and hours of experience and stuffed arrow after arrow into our quiver by the time our golden opportunity comes along.

The Victor Dakin Opportunity

If luck can be defined as "when preparedness meets opportunity," then my good luck in the horse game started out in the form of a letter from Jane Schemilt one late winter day in 1973.

Jane, from Quebec, was taking courses in commercial photography at the Doscher School of Photography in South Woodstock, Vermont. In her letter Jane explained that as the new career demanded her full commitment, she had reluctantly decided to sell her ten-year-old eventing partner, Victor Dakin, and would I be interested?

Victor had gone Advanced a few times, was fast and brave and a good jumper, but was very difficult in dressage. His price, five thousand dollars, was expensive for those days—but not exceptionally so for an upper-level horse, even one that had the potential to get hot and worried on the flat.

May and I decided to drive right up to Cowansville, Quebec, to see him, and I called Allen Leslie to see whether he could fly up to Burlington, Vermont, so that we could pick him up on our way to the farm where Victor was spending the winter. We figured that as an experienced equine vet, Allen could do a pre-purchase exam right on the spot. Looking back

Laura Graves with Verdades ("Diddy"), who she co-owns with partner Curt Maes and trained from a foal, was the first American dressage rider to be ranked #1 on the FEI World Ranking List. She won team bronze at the 2016 Olympics in Rio de Janeiro and team gold and individual silver at the Pan American Games in 2015.

Laura Graves and Verdades at the 2019 World Equestrian Games in Tryon, North Carolina, where they won two silver medals. Laura and her family found "Diddy" when he was six months old and she trained him up through the levels.

Discipline: Dressage

In 2014, Laura was fourth at the World Equestrian Games in Normandie, France, and in 2015, she was fourth in the World Cup Final in Las Vegas, Nevada. At the World Cup (Omaha) in 2017, she came in second, and she and Diddy had another second-place finish in the World Cup (Paris) in 2018. Laura won two more silver medals at the World Equestrian Games (Tryon, North Carolina) in 2018, and achieved a second-place finish at the 2019 World Cup Final in Gothenburg, Sweden.

Life circumstances:

I grew up in a very small town in Vermont with my parents and two sisters. We spent a lot of time outdoors and were fortunate enough to always have animals in our lives—dogs and cats. When we were very small, there were also horses. Our first two ponies came from a rather odd business deal that my father made with some family friends. He was working at a hardware store at the time, and the family friends offered him two ponies in exchange for my family's used washer and dryer. My dad thought this was a great idea seeing as he could get a new washer and dryer at a very good price! From there, having two ponies turned into rescuing horses here and there, and even breeding one of our own.

Hooked on horses when:

By middle school my sisters had focused more on "standard" sports, like soccer and tennis and basketball. My parents, seeing how serious I was about horses, made the commitment to buy me my first "real" horse. This was a four-year-old Quarter Horse named Sunny that we found in Canada. At that time in my life I wanted to be an eventer, but I ended up having quite a bit of fear, and as it turned out I was good at dressage! By the time I had reached high school, dressage was my main focus, but it was clear that Sunny's abilities were limited and me "slowing down" in my pursuit of the top the sport was not on the radar. My parents made another commitment to my goals, and we were able to purchase my current top horse, Verdades, as a foal in 2002.

I think I got good because:

⌁ I got good because there was no other choice. Whatever responsibility we had, my parents made sure that we gave it our best efforts.

⌁ I got good because I got good at failing. I got comfortable with never winning and never being on top…and I never let it kill my fire but rather fuel it.

⌁ Most importantly, I am fortunate enough to be surrounded by people who support me and love me unconditionally.

My most important advice:

My most important advice in this industry is to figure out why you're doing it…and stay true to that. It's so easy to see the grass as being greener on the other side, and you will quickly lose your love of the sport, and more importantly, your love of horses. If you can maintain the love and the motivation that made you pursue a career in horses in the first place, then there is nothing holding you back from true success.

Laura Graves

on that moment from thirty-six years later, I think I must have been pretty sure I was going to buy Victor before we even got in the car.

I remember that there was less and less snow as we drove north, but the little Quonset hut indoor arena where I tried him had ice across about a quarter of the floor—it was jump the fence, land, and hit the brakes to avoid skating into the wall. Luckily I'd seen Victor compete enough to give me more to go on than the little I could see and feel that day, so we decided to buy him.

What "arrows" did I have in my "quiver" when this opportunity surfaced in my life?

By the time I got the letter from Jane Schemilt, I was about to begin my twentieth season of competitive riding—and my experience included more than eventing.

I'd been the gymkhana champion of Western Massachusetts in 1955. I'd shown Morgans at the National Morgan Horse Show in the mid-1950s. I'd already ridden in nine 100-Mile Trail Rides at the Green Mountain Horse Association between 1956 and 1966. I'd been eventing for eleven years. I'd taken my first event horse, Lighting Magic, through the Intermediate three-day level and I'd taken both House Guest and Cat through Advanced. Additionally, I'd jumped House Guest five-foot-ten and Cat six feet in horse shows. In other words, I had sat on a lot of different horses and done a lot of different things.

I couldn't know that Victor Dakin would prove to be one of the most reliable Advanced cross-country machines in the world for the next six years, giving me clear round after clear round, including a 1974 World Championship gold-medal round, a USET National Three-Day Championship clear round at the 1976 Radnor Horse Trials in Pennsylvania, and a clear round at the 1977 Ledyard International Event in Massachusetts, all of which positioned me to become fully involved from then on as a coach, teacher, and trainer.

So great was Victor's influence on my competitive career and subsequent full-time involvement with horses that May and I have often half joked that our farm should be named Victor Dakin Farm instead of Tamarack Hill Farm. How sad it would have been to miss a once-in-a-lifetime opportunity, like that letter from Jane Schemilt, because I hadn't done my part by filling my quiver with the arrows I needed.

A quiver full of arrows is a must if you're aiming for the very top of your discipline, but choosing to put those arrows in there is also essential if your goal is more about getting to be a *better* rider than about becoming *the best* rider. By making the choices that enable you to add those arrows, you equip yourself for a sense of accomplishment and self-fulfillment. If you come home with a blue ribbon, you may have won it at a national competition or at some small regional show, but by goodness it's hanging on your wall and it's a lift! If you know you've accomplished something significant, you don't need to worry about whether the world recognizes it. You have made the choices that enabled you to produce this result, and now you can choose to give yourself the credit you deserve.

The one thing that finally matters is for each of you to decide where you want to go and how far you want to get in this quest to become good at riding, good at driving horses, or just good *with* horses. Realize, too, that you can always modify those decisions and make different choices later—most of them, anyway. If you've chosen to have three children, that's probably not a choice you can undo!

Then, once you've made your decisions, use *How Good Riders Get Good* as an atlas and road map. Study how the twenty-three good riders and drivers who shared their stories within these pages made *their* choices—not all the same choices by any means, but right for each of them.

If you get confused by the thicket of choices, read this book again, or portions of it, and look for signposts to aim yourself in the right direction. Remember, the "right direction" is only right if the choices you make are the best ones for *you*.

Good Rider Recommended Reading List

To go from "Wannabe" to "Gonnabe" and learn to deal with the cards you hold:

That Winning Feeling and *It's Not Just About the Ribbons* by Jane Savoie

To help appreciate the teachers, mentors, and extended support team necessary for riding success:

Instant Replay: The Green Bay Packers Diary of Jerry Kramer by Jerry Kramer

To better your body and better your ability to *use* your body in the saddle:

The Riding Docter by Dr. Beth Glosten

Centered Riding and *Centered Riding 2* by Sally Swift

To see the nine character traits of a successful rider at work in others:

The Headmaster by John McPhee

How to Win Friends and Influence People by Dale Carnegie

Mastery: The Keys to Success and Long-Term Fulfillment by George Burr Leonard

Winning with Frank Chapot by Frank Chapot

Reflections on Riding and Jumping by William Steinkraus

Outliers: The Story of Success by Malcolm Gladwell

Gallop to Freedom by Magali Delgado and Frédéric Pignon

To successfully navigate the vast sea of horse knowledge:

Training the Three-Day Event Horse and Rider by James Wofford

Gymnastics: Systematic Training for Jumping Horses by James Wofford

Hunter Seat Equitation by George Morris

The All-Around Horse and Rider by Donna Snyder-Smith

Horse and Rider by Judy Richter

Intermediate Dressage by RLV Ffrench Blake

The Event Groom's Handbook by Jeanne Kane and Lisa Waltman

Dressage Riding by Richard L. Watjen

The Horse's Pain-Free Back and Saddle-Fit Book and *The Western Horse's Pain-Free Back and Saddle-Fit Book* by Joyce Harman, DVM, MRCVS

Cavalletti by Reiner Klimke and Ingrid Klimke

Beyond the Track by Anna Morgan Ford & Amber Heintzberger

Photo Credits

Courtesy of Denny Emerson: pp. 2, 10, 12, 14 (inset), 28, 30, 51, 66, 76, 84, 86, 100, 104, 110, 116, 129, 134, 166, 172, 177, 179

©Diana De Rosa Photography: pp. 6, 102, 168, 180

Carol Fenwick: p. 14 (main photo)

Courtesy of Anne Gribbons: p. 24

Mary Phelps: p. 27

Shannon Brinkman: pp. 32, 46, 190

From the book *Reining Essentials* by Sandy Collier and used by permission: p. 36

©TIEC: p. 48

Sve Stickle: p. 58

Abby Rowlee Photography (inset); Nicole Parker (main): p. 64

Robin Duncan: p. 74

Ashley Yanke: p. 80

Rhett Savoie: p. 90

Amber Heintzberger: p. 98

Pamela Burton: p. 114

Kimberly Chason: p. 118

Mike J. McNally: pp. 126, 160

Jenni Autry: p. 140

Kelly Lemenze: p. 144

Lolisa Monroe: p. 150

AlixColeman.com: p. 174

Index

Page numbers in *italics* indicate figures.